W9-BZX-317

COOKING WILD
KATE'S IN CAMP

DELICIOUS EASY-TO-FIX RECIPES FOR CAMP, CABIN OR TRAIL

BY KATE FIDUCCIA

CREATIVE
PUBLISHING
international

CHANHASSEN, MINNESOTA

www.creativepub.com

DEDICATION

This book is dedicated to my husband, Peter, and our son, Cody, who always give their faithful support for all my endeavors, endure my experimental dishes and recipes whipped up on a whim, and reliably leave me room in the goose blind.

President/CEO: Michael Eleftheriou
Vice President/Publisher: Linda Ball

Cooking Wild in Kate's Camp
by Kate Fiduccia

Executive Editor, Outdoor Products Group: David R. Maas
Managing Editor: Jill Anderson
Editor: Teresa Marrone
Creative Director: Bradley Springer
Photographer: Tate Carlson
Assistant Photographer: Herb Schnabel
Studio Manager: Jeanette Moss McCurdy
Food and Prop Stylist: Abby Wyckoff
Assistant Food Stylist: Susan Telleen
Director, Production Services: Kim Gerber
Production Staff: Stephanie Barakos, Laura Hokkanen, Helga Thielen

Some images © 2001-2002 www.arttoday.com

Printing: R. R. Donnelley & Sons Co.
10 9 8 7 6 5 4 3 2 1

Library of Congress Cataloging-in-Publication Data

Fiduccia, Kate.
  Cooking wild in Kate's camp : delicious easy-to-fix recipes for camp, cabin or trail / by Kate Fiduccia.
      p. cm. – (Freshwater angler) (The complete hunter)
    ISBN 1-58923-040-X
    1. Outdoor cookery. 2. Cookery (Game). 3. Quick and easy cookery. I. Title. II. Series III. Complete hunter (Creative Publishing International)
    TX823 .F52 2002
    641.5'78–dc21

                                    2002025709

TABLE OF CONTENTS

Introduction

*M*y love of outdoor cooking has been developed through nearly two decades of hunting and fishing across North America. As co-host of the Woods N' Waters TV series, I've been fortunate to visit some of the finest spots around. From the back-country streams in New York's Adirondack Mountains to the aspen-filled valleys of northern Utah, my travels have allowed me to cook in some of the most beautiful settings on earth. Along the way, I've also been privileged to savor bounty prepared by fellow anglers and hunters.

In the following pages, you'll find over 140 of my quick, simple, delicious recipes for a variety of fish and wild game. For the most part, the main ingredients in these recipes will be shot or landed at camp. But there are also some non-game recipes for those times you'll be carrying things like ground beef to camp. In addition, you'll see easy-to-fix recipes for breads, beverages and vegetable dishes to supplement the wild fare. I've even included some gems generously shared by outfitters and guides I've encountered over the years, as well as by other folks for whom the outdoors and Mother Nature's bounty are a major passion. I know you'll enjoy their contributions as well.

Each recipe in this book includes approximate preparation time, nutritional information and helpful hints, such as pre-measuring and pre-mixing ingredients when packing. And because I bet that some of these recipes will become family standards, I'll give you a tip: You don't have to be miles from nowhere to prepare these dishes. For instance, your backyard grill will work just as well as a campfire for most of the recipes that call for cooking over coals.

Here is a brief summary of the cooking methods described for each recipe in this book:

For Stovetop or Surface Cooking: These recipes can be cooked on almost any heat source available—on a camp stove or traditional range, over a campfire, or even using a hot plate. All require some sort of pot or skillet.

For Cooking Over Coals: This method is for campfires made with either deadwood or charcoal briquettes; a grill grate is sometimes needed to keep the food away from direct contact with the coals. Most of these dishes can also be cooked on a regular charcoal or propane grill.

For Camp or Home Cooking in an Oven: These recipes are for preparation in a regular oven (whether at camp or at home) or a woodstove. Baking temperatures must be controlled and monitored fairly closely. You'll need standard baking pans or casserole dishes.

For Camp or Home Cooking with a Broiler: Look for these recipes if your cabin has a regular cooking range with a broiler, or if you are preparing dishes at home. There is no substitute method for broiling.

For Dutch Oven Cooking: Unlike the large stove-top kettle of the same name, the true Dutch oven is a special cast-iron pot that has feet to hold it above a small bed of coals. It also features a rimmed lid that is designed to hold coals, so the food inside cooks from both the top and the bottom. Dutch oven cookery is traditionally done with red-hot coals in a campfire setting, but you can also use the Dutch oven with a woodstove.

There's something about a full day's hike in the mountains that makes you crave hearty food. When you're so hungry, it seems that everything would taste good. But that doesn't mean you have to settle for hot dogs on a stick every time. Yes, it is possible to fish, hunt or hike all day and still enjoy a mouth-watering camp meal, and this book will show you how.

Tips for Getting Started

PLANNING AHEAD

When planning meals for your trip, remember your limitations. First of all, most of what you pack in, you must pack out, and this includes garbage such as empty cans, plastic containers, etc. Plan your meals carefully to avoid carrying too much food, or too little. Your selection of food items will also vary depending upon the size of your party, the way you'll be carrying gear, and whether you are cooking with a backpacker's stove, a woodstove or over a campfire. It's easy to pack food and gear for a short weekend fishing trip into a medium-sized backpack; in contrast, food and gear for a week-long elk hunt is often packed in on horseback.

I prefer fresh food on the trail whenever I can manage it. Fresh fruits and vegetables are a good staple to carry, but many have a short shelf life and must be packed carefully to avoid bruising (which can hasten decay). Fresh meats must be kept cool or frozen and should be prepared early in the trip. Fresh dairy products are essential as well. Eggs must be kept cool, but can be transported in no-break plastic containers. Cheese is an excellent source of protein, calories and calcium. I like to take large blocks of both cheddar and Parmesan. This way, the cheeses can be freshly grated for recipes or toppings, and can also be sliced for appetizers; the remainder can be re-wrapped and stored away for later use.

Many camping staples require no refrigeration. Freeze-dried vegetables, fruits and meats are lightweight, last for the duration of even long trips, and reconstitute well in soups and stews. Powdered milk can be reconstituted and used in cooking and for drinking, and evaporated milk works well, too (although the cans are bulky). Dried staples such as beans and rice won't spoil, but often require lengthy cooking times.

I feel it is essential to take the time to plan out the food items, day by day, and then make a list of ingredients needed for each day. This will make packing and storing so much easier. In addition, should the camp cook not be able to carry out his/her duties on any given day, the replacement chef will have a much easier time filling in. It will lessen the stress for everyone to know that everything has been outlined and detailed. This way, when you return to your duties, the "chaos" you might expect to find will be minimal.

Whether on a short 2-day backpacking trip or a longer unnecessary trip, I like to label and group food items in plastic zipper-style bags. For example, I portion out pancake mix in one small plastic bag and label it "Pancakes B-1" for Breakfast, Day One. I place this bag and another small plastic bag with dehydrated peaches, labeled "Peaches B-1," in a larger bag labeled "B-1." I also add a few hot cocoa packets to the same bag. This way, when it comes time to prepare that breakfast, I don't have to fish around for multiple food items – I just grab the single bag.

I like to chop, slice or dice as many food items ahead of time as possible. When shopping for canned items, look for those in convenient forms – chopped mushrooms, sliced olives, etc. Dry items like breading, seasoned flour and cake mix can be pre-mixed at home, placed in a plastic bag and labeled accordingly. In addition, dressings, marinades and sauces can also be mixed ahead of time and placed in plastic containers.

KEEPING FOOD FRESH AND COOL

The type of trip, length of your trip and the number of folks in your party will determine the number and type of coolers that you bring. Sometimes, if we plan on camping for more than 4 days, we'll pack an extra cooler that is taped shut and will not be opened until the fourth day. The other coolers are labeled according to what is inside; items that require the most refrigeration and are the most perishable are kept at the bottom of the cooler. If you're camping with kids, keep one cooler filled with drinks and reserve another for the more perishable items. Try to regulate who can go in and out of the beverage cooler to keep it from being opened too frequently.

Anything that will be in a cooler should be either frozen or well chilled before packing. Bottled water that is at room temperature will warm up the frozen or cooled items next to it. Remember that block ice lasts longer than crushed ice, and can be chipped as needed for drinks. Reusable "blue ice" packs keep things cold and don't make messy meltwater as they warm up, but also must be carried back out after their usefulness has passed.

If you are going to be on a longer trip, pack perishable food items in the cooler(s) according to when they will be used. Always remember to minimize the number of times you'll be going into the cooler. If circumstances allow, it's a good idea to keep one cooler for the day's meals, and another as the main storage cooler. In the morning, transfer all food items from the main cooler to the day's cooler. Then, re-seal the main cooler and keep it in the coolest place at your campsite for the day.

COOK STOVES

If you'll be camping in a high-use spot, or an area that offers little natural wood for campfires, a gas-powered camping stove can save the day. Powered by white gas, butane, propane or kerosene, a modern camp stove will usually last many days, particularly when supplemented with a charcoal or natural wood fire. In my experience, white gas, often called Coleman fuel, is one of the best fuel sources for camp stoves.

If your camp has a woodstove, you are in for a real treat. Woodstoves offer a luxury to the camp cook. With the proper knowledge of its setup, fueling and cleaning, you can enjoy fresh baked breads, slow-simmered stews, and mouth-watering roasted meats from the kitchen range. If the woodstove you will be using has not been in full-time use, check the chimney to see if there are any nesting birds or furred animals. An easy way to check the chimney is to place a mirror into the chimney opening. If there are no problems, you'll be able to see daylight from the top of the pipe down (unless the pipe has multiple bends). If you don't see any light, you had better find out what's causing the obstruction before lighting a fire.

Although almost any cookware will work with a woodstove, cast-iron griddles, Dutch ovens, and skillets are the preferred cooking utensils. They cook evenly, withstand a lot of abuse and require little maintenance. Other cookware will work, too, but be careful of plastic or metal handles as they will absorb heat from the stove.

For more information on woodstove use, see the sidebars on pages 48-49, and 58.

DUTCH OVENS

If you are able to bring one of these old-fashioned cooking pots to camp, you will love its versatility. It serves a multitude of purposes and can function as your one pot at camp. A decent-sized Dutch oven can be used as a skillet, a griddle, a stew pot, and an oven. Most camp Dutch ovens are made of cast iron, although some are made from heavy-duty aluminum. They vary in size from 8 to 24 inches across, with depths ranging from 4 to 6 inches. Most Dutch ovens have three legs that allow them to be set right over the fire or charcoal briquettes. To use the utensil as an oven, preheat the rimmed lid, place it on top of the base and arrange briquettes on top of the lid. This way heat is passed into the Dutch oven from both the top and the bottom. You can bake some delicious breads, meals and desserts in this black "cauldron."

Like all cast-iron cookware, Dutch ovens should be seasoned, at home, prior to cooking. Seasoning prevents the oven from rusting and also creates a nonstick surface. To season cast-iron cookware: Wash the utensil with soap and water to remove any dirt or residue from shipping. Dry the entire piece. Next, coat the inside, outside and lid with nonsalted shortening such as Crisco. Place in a 350°F oven for about 1 hour. Keep the windows open as the shortening will smoke − and seep out through the oven doors. Once the pot has cooled, wipe out any excess grease. You're now ready for cooking. The nonstick surface improves as you use the pot, and eventually it will have an almost silky sheen.

Once the Dutch oven has been seasoned, you must clean it properly after each use. Scrape out any food particles with a rubber spatula, and wash the piece in plain, hot water. Never use soap or you may have to season the oven again. Dry the pot either over a warm fire or on a stove, then wipe a thin coating of oil over the inside and outside.

When you want to use the Dutch oven as an oven rather than just as a large pot, a good rule of thumb that I learned from an excellent camp cook in Wyoming is "plus two for the top and minus two for the bottom." For instance, if you have an 8-inch Dutch oven, use 10 briquettes on the top (8 plus 2) and 6 on the bottom (8 minus 2). Remember to start the briquettes 20 to 30 minutes in advance, so that they are gray along the edges. See pages 10 and 11 of this book for a photo sequence on how to properly use a Dutch oven.

CAMPFIRES

Presuming that there is not a fire site already designated at your camping area, keep these factors in mind when choosing your site. Keep the fire site at least 20 feet from tents, gear, surrounding vegetation or anything else that is flammable. Don't build your campfire on top of ground that harbors roots near the surface. Fire can burn in an underground root system and flare up as a wildfire away from the campsite. Clear the area of all twigs, brush, leaves, needles, etc.; the fire site should be bare earth. If you dig a pit for the fire, be sure to save the chunk of earth, and replace it before you leave camp.

If there is a choice of bringing charcoal or using deadwood, remember that charcoal briquettes offer more consistent heat over a longer period. Charcoal also produces less ash residue than a wood fire.

An excellent way to minimize your fire impact is to build your fire inside a firepan. A firepan is a round or square piece of metal that is generally 12 to 18 inches across, with rimmed sides of 3 to 4 inches. You could use an oil drip pan from the auto parts store or even an old charcoal grill base. The purpose of the firepan is to contain the fire and also avoid scarring the ground with the marks of your fire (if you raise the firepan off the ground with some rocks, or place it on a bed of sand, the marking will be minimized even further). A firepan also helps control the size of your fire. And, firepans are great for Dutch ovens, as they contain the fire around the Dutch oven.

Whether cooking with a firepan or not, be sure to surround the fire with large rocks to enclose it. But be sure to avoid rocks such as shale or other moisture-holding river rocks that might explode once heated by the fire!

Under ideal conditions in good weather, use deadwood that has already fallen to the ground. Should you be setting up camp during a rainstorm, however, standing deadwood is a better choice. More often than not, the middle of the log will be quite dry and is much easier to start a fire with than the wet deadwood on the ground. Never cut live vegetation for firewood. Cutting live vegetation is not a wise use of our natural resources, and in some places it is illegal. Moreover, when green wood is used in fires, it does not burn as hot as dead or dried wood. Green wood carries a tremendous amount of moisture. When it's burning, more energy is spent getting the moisture out of the wood than is spent producing cooking or heating energy.

Firewood that is larger than your forearm is too big for cooking purposes. Also, the standard rule when afield is to gather twice as much wood as you think you'll need. Many inexperienced campers are often surprised at how much wood will be used during one evening's campfire. Good sources of tinder (to light the kindling) include dried birch bark, old birds' nests, sagebrush bark, mesquite branches, and dead twigs from pine trees.

Never use gasoline or any other fuel to start a fire or even to hurry a fire along. This could be dangerous and might cause more than an unpleasant taste to your meal. Never leave a fire unattended. It only takes a quick gust of wind to either get the fire going

out of control or send ashes to other areas of the campsite where much more damage could occur. Always keep a bucket of water and a shovel near the fire in case it unexpectedly gets out of control.

When the fire has burned completely down, stir in a small amount of liquid to extinguish whatever smoldering embers are left. If you are going to leave your campsite and travel far from it for the day, make sure the fire is put out well in advance of your departure to ensure it truly has been extinguished and there are no hot embers.

ALUMINUM FOIL

Foil is an excellent cooking tool when afield. Sealed foil packages work almost like a pressure cooker in that the steam is captured inside and the food cooks rapidly. Some of those who cook with foil cover a bed of red-hot coals with ash and then place the foil packet on the ash. Others prefer to clear an area in a bed of red-hot coals bare to the ground or the bottom of the firepan, place the foil package down and shovel the hot coals back over the top. Both methods require that you turn the package about halfway through the cooking process. I like to use a double layer of foil; the outer one collects the sooty ash and can sustain a minor tear when turned with a green stick, while the inside layer is much cleaner and can also serve as a dish, if needed.

When cooking vegetables or potatoes in a foil packet, remember to leave some air space when wrapping the package. This way, the steam will help cook the vegetables. For added flavor, it's always good to add a little butter or margarine when cooking drier items. Also, a foil packet of potatoes or onions can also be placed at the hot edge of the fire to cook while you're using the main source of the fire to cook something else. Remember that potatoes usually require about an hour to cook.

COOKING UTENSILS

Bring along cooking utensils that serve multiple purposes. For example, I like to bring along a slotted spoon that can also serve as a colander when draining items either from a can or from a pot. Metal cooking utensils are sturdy, won't melt and can be sterilized quickly in the fire. A good spatula and spoon are the minimum tools needed. But, I also like to pack a multi-purpose can/bottle opener/cork screw, a small folding saw and knife, long-handled tongs, a Dutch oven lid lifter, and a giant, long-handled fork for roasting hot dogs or apples.

BREAKFAST
CAMP RECIPES

*N*ot one of us has grown up without hearing Mother say, "Breakfast is the most important meal of the day." A truer statement Mom never made, especially when it comes to camping out. A warm, hearty breakfast can set the tone for the day and give you the energy you'll need to hike the extra mile, climb a few hundred feet higher or have the stamina to stay out all day. While the rest of the day's meals certainly provide additional nutrition, none is as important to the camper as breakfast.

This old adage was brought home to me during one of our most recent hunting trips in central Saskatchewan, Canada. The outfitter's daughter, Taba, was the cook. Each morning, she prepared a rib-sticking breakfast and encouraged everyone to finish the very last morsel on his or her plate. The first morning, I was busy preparing the video and audio equipment for our television series Woods N' Waters and I needed extra time to tape handwarmers to the batteries in order to extend their life as much as possible in the bitter −20°F winds. I didn't have time to eat a full breakfast and, instead, quickly drank a cup of Chai tea and nibbled at a warm sweet bun.

I paid dearly for this mistake. At first light, we saw what would later turn out to be the largest whitetail either Peter or I had ever seen on the hoof. Another hunter, who was returning to camp early because of the cold weather, inadvertently jumped the big buck from its bedding area. The buck was a few hundred yards away and we watched the snow fly up from its feet as it made a beeline across the field to the next woodlot − or "bush" as it is referred to in Saskatchewan. I had never seen Peter so excited. He immediately planned his strategy to take the buck, deciding to wait an hour or two on the hillside that overlooked the woodlot. While he glassed over one area, the outfitters glassed over another. After 45 minutes of waiting patiently, I began to shiver. Soon I was shaking uncontrollably, and that was the end of our shoot for the day. We gave up our plan and returned to camp. If only I had eaten a more substantial breakfast that morning, I'm sure I would have had enough energy to remain on stand and in the field for as long as it took.

Oh, yes, about the buck. Peter did eventually take this monster whitetail − three days later − on a day when I was smart enough to eat as much breakfast as I could comfortably handle. The 16-point buck scored an unbelievable 207 3/8 B&C points, non-typical.

The following recipes will stick to your ribs and provide hearty sustenance for the day ahead. Some, like Outback Hashbrowns, are traditional camp fare, while others provide some great ideas for using leftover fish or game for a filling start to the day.

OUTBACK HASHBROWNS

One of my favorite foods to have left over in camp is bacon. It adds delicious flavor to almost any recipe — breakfast, lunch or dinner — and its aroma lends woodsy ambience to the meal. When I have leftover bacon, I often plan on Outback Hashbrowns for the next morning.

<u>Serves:</u> 2
<u>Cooking Time:</u> Under 30 minutes

- 2 tablespoons vegetable oil
- 1 large onion, chopped
- 2 large potatoes, diced with skins on
- 1/2 cup water
- 3 slices cooked bacon, chopped
     Salt and pepper

<u>For Stovetop or Surface Cooking:</u> In medium skillet, heat oil over medium heat. Add onion and cook until slightly colored. Add potatoes and water. Cook for 10 to 15 minutes, or until most of the water has cooked away. Add the bacon and cook an additional 5 minutes to heat thoroughly and blend flavors. Season with salt and pepper to taste.

VENISON HASH

This is one of my long-time favorite breakfast camp recipes. It is versatile and can go from a simple patty to a stand-alone McMuffin-style meal with minimal effort (especially when lunch may be postponed because of good fishing!). For those who like their food spicy, a few drops of red or green Tabasco sauce will weave some magic into this already mouth-watering meal.

<u>Serves:</u> 4
<u>Cooking Time:</u> Under 15 minutes

- 1 lb. leftover venison roast, diced
- 4 medium leftover cooked potatoes, diced
- 1 small onion, diced
- 1 egg, beaten
- 1/4 teaspoon salt
- 1/8 teaspoon garlic powder
- 1/8 teaspoon pepper
- 2 tablespoons vegetable oil
- 2 teaspoons maple syrup or a few dashes of Tabasco sauce

<u>For Stovetop or Surface Cooking:</u> In a large bowl, mix the venison, potatoes, onion, egg, salt, garlic powder and pepper. Shape into patties about 1/2 inch thick. Heat oil in large skillet over medium heat. Cook patties about 2 minutes on the first side. Flip patties and drizzle a little maple syrup on the cooked side; or, for the more daring, sprinkle some Tabasco on top of each patty. Cook second side for about 2 minutes longer.

Carrying Vegetables to Camp

☞ *Any time I bring vegetables on a camping trip that'll be longer than a few days, I try to use them early on in the trip in order to maximize their flavor and nutritional value. No matter what type of container you pack veggies in, any significant elevation in storage temperature can wreak havoc with them. Also, remember that some vegetables should not be stored together. For example, onions should not be stored with potatoes, as gasses from the onions will cause the potatoes to spoil more quickly.*

DUTCH OVEN STICKY BUNS

This recipe can bring your "home kitchen" to the outdoors. I've yet to meet anyone who wasn't mesmerized by the aroma and flavor of sticky buns in camp!

<u>*Yield:*</u> 9 or 10 buns, to serve 4
<u>*Cooking Time:*</u> 30 to 60 minutes

Filling mixture:
1/2 cup sugar
1/4 cup chopped walnuts
1/4 cup raisins
  2 tablespoons cinnamon

Dough mixture:
11/2 cups buttermilk baking mix
  2 tablespoons powdered buttermilk

  3 tablespoons butter, softened
1/3 cup cold water

    You will also need: Plastic wrap, Dutch oven, parchment paper

<u>*Optional Advance Preparation:*</u> In small zipper-style bag, combine filling-mixture ingredients. In larger bag, combine dough-mixture ingredients.

<u>*For Dutch Oven Cooking:*</u> Prepare campfire; preheat Dutch oven lid in coals. Add butter to bag with filling mixture. Mix together in bag; set aside. Add water to bag with dough mixture; knead well. When thoroughly mixed, remove from bag and place on clean, flat work surface covered with plastic wrap. Spread dough out to a square about 10 inches across and about 1/4 inch thick. (A wine bottle works well as a rolling pin; in a pinch, you can press the dough out with your fingertips.) Sprinkle filling mixture over flattened dough. Using plastic wrap to lift and manipulate dough, roll dough into a log (but don't roll the plastic wrap into the log). Cut log into 1-inch portions.

Line bottom of Dutch oven with parchment paper cut to fit the bottom; this will prevent the buns from sticking. Place buns on parchment side by side, cut side down. Place preheated lid on Dutch oven. Position Dutch oven over small bed of coals; place 10 to 12 hot coals on top of lid. Bake for 15 to 20 minutes. Remove from oven and let cool before serving.

<u>*For Camp or Home Cooking in an Oven:*</u> Heat oven to 350°F. Prepare rolls as directed above, arranging on ungreased baking sheet. Bake for 10 to 15 minutes. Let cool before serving.

How to Use a Dutch Oven

1. Build a campfire, or start charcoal briquettes. Let fire burn down to glowing coals. If specified in recipe, preheat Dutch oven lid in coals (see photo above).

2. Assemble ingredients in Dutch oven as directed in recipe, then place Dutch oven over a small bed of 6 to 8 glowing coals. Cover with lid.

continued on page 11

KICK-START OATMEAL

This is one of my own personal favorites. I'm a big lover of berries and nuts of all kinds, and this recipe incorporates them both. There is one problem, however: This can be addictive (so to speak)!

<u>*Serves:*</u> 2
<u>*Cooking Time:*</u> Under 15 minutes

1¹/₂ cups cold water	1/4 cup fresh blueberries
2/3 cup old-fashioned oatmeal	1/4 cup walnuts
1/2 cup raisins	Honey for serving
2 tablespoons brown sugar	

<u>*For Stovetop or Surface Cooking:*</u> In small pot, heat water to boiling over medium-high heat. Add oatmeal, stirring constantly to prevent it from clumping together. Cook for about 5 minutes, stirring frequently. Add raisins; cook and stir for about 2 minutes longer. Remove from heat and stir in the brown sugar, blueberries and walnuts. Divide between 2 bowls and drizzle a little honey on top of each serving.

CATSKILL CORN PATTIES

I don't know anyone who doesn't like corn bread, and these tasty corn pancakes are equally satisfying. Served with an accompaniment such as scrambled eggs or wild berry compote, they hit the mark. If you prepare all the ingredients at home, they're especially quick and easy to make.

<u>*Yield:*</u> 9 2-inch patties
<u>*Cooking Time:*</u> Under 30 minutes

Corn patty mixture:
 1 package (7 oz.) corn bread mix
 2 tablespoons powdered milk
 1 tablespoon powdered egg

1/3 cup water
 1 tablespoon honey
 1 tablespoon vegetable oil

<u>*Optional Advance Preparation:*</u> Combine corn-patty mixture in a plastic food-storage bag.

<u>*For Stovetop or Surface Cooking:*</u> Add water and honey to corn-patty mixture in the bag; knead well to smooth out any lumps. In medium skillet, heat oil over low heat. If you have plenty of bags, cut a small hole in the corner to pipe out the batter into the skillet. If the bag is to be re-used, spoon batter into skillet in 2-tablespoon portions. Let patties cook until bubbles appear on surface. Flip patties and cook until golden on second side. Keep warm in a towel while you prepare remaining patties.

3. Scoop 12 to 15 glowing coals onto the lid of the Dutch oven and cook as directed. Check the coals periodically and replenish if necessary.

4. Be careful when opening the lid to check for doneness. Brush ashes from the edges of the lid to prevent them from falling into the pot when you open it (see photo above).

GOBBLER OMELET

One of my favorite wild game meats is turkey. Combined with the ingredients in this recipe, it will make you want to "Gobble, Gobble" — get it? This goes well with Catskill Corn Patties (page 11).

<u>*Serves:*</u> 2
<u>*Cooking Time:*</u> Under 30 minutes

  2 slices bacon, chopped
     Half of a small onion, chopped
  1 cup chopped leftover cooked turkey meat
1/8 teaspoon cayenne pepper
     Salt and pepper
  5 eggs
  1 tablespoon water
  1 tablespoon butter, divided
1/2 cup shredded cheddar cheese, divided

<u>*For Stovetop or Surface Cooking:*</u> In medium skillet* or Dutch oven, cook bacon over medium heat until beginning to crisp. When it is almost done, add onion and cook until soft. Add turkey meat and season with cayenne pepper, and salt and pepper to taste. Transfer turkey mixture to a dish and cover, or wrap in foil to keep warm; wipe the skillet clean.

In medium bowl, combine eggs and 1 tablespoon water. Beat gently with fork until just blended; over-beating will make the omelet rubbery. Melt half of the butter in cleaned skillet over medium heat. When butter begins to sizzle, add half of the egg mixture, tilting pan to spread eggs over bottom. As soon as the eggs begin to set on the bottom, pull cooked egg from the edge with a wooden spoon and tilt the pan to let the liquid egg flow into the space. Continue to cook and repeat the last step until most of the liquid egg has been cooked.

Sprinkle half of the cooked turkey mixture and half of the cheese over one half of the omelet (like a half-moon). Tilt the skillet to one side and fold over the "empty" half of the omelet with a spatula. To make sure all the cheese has melted, place a lid on the skillet for about 30 seconds. Remove the cover and transfer omelet to individual plate. Cook the second omelet in the same manner as the first.

<u>*Note:*</u> If you are using a large skillet, you can cook 1 large omelet rather than 2 individual omelets. Proceed as directed, using all of the ingredients at once.

Eggs

☞ *Egg dishes and omelets taste best when made with fresh eggs. However, since fresh eggs can be bulky and heavy, many campers and backpackers use freeze-dried or powdered eggs. While freeze-dried eggs cost a bit more than powdered eggs, they taste much better. One way to improve the taste of freeze-dried eggs is adding some fresh wild onions or garlic, or combining fresh and dried eggs. You need just 1 fresh egg in a 4-egg omelet to make it taste a lot better.*

VEGETARIAN PITA DELIGHT

While the eggs are cooking, I often thread a green stick through a pita pocket and singe the outside over the fire, making it warm and crispy. The resulting meal is tasty and nutritious.

Serves: 4
Cooking Time: Under 30 minutes

3 tablespoons vegetable oil, divided	1 teaspoon crumbled dried oregano
1 large onion, chopped	1/4 teaspoon salt
2 tomatoes, seeded and chopped	6 eggs, lightly beaten
1 green bell pepper, cored and chopped	2 tablespoons water
	2 large or 4 small pita rounds

For Stovetop or Surface Cooking: In skillet or Dutch oven, heat 2 tablespoons of the oil over high heat. Add onion and cook until translucent but not brown. Lower heat and add tomatoes, bell pepper, oregano and salt. Stir and let simmer for about 15 minutes. Add eggs and 2 tablespoons water to pan and cook without stirring until eggs begin to set. Stir and continue cooking until the eggs are done. Cut 2 large pitas in half, or cut off the tops of 4 smaller pitas; open pitas gently. Spoon cooked egg mixture into opened pitas and serve immediately.

STEAK 'N' FRIED EGGS

One of my husband's favorite meals is steak and eggs. During an elk hunt in Montana, one of the hunters in our party shot a cow elk and was generous enough to share some venison with us. I rustled up this dish the following morning, while some of the hunters were waiting out a rainstorm. As the aroma permeated the cook tent, it drew in the hunters like a magnet.

Serves: 4
Cooking Time: Under 15 minutes

1 lb. venison loin (deer, moose or elk), trimmed of all fat and connective tissue	1/4 cup butter (half of a stick), divided
Salt and pepper	2 medium onions, chopped
	4 eggs

For Stovetop or Surface Cooking: Cut loin into steaks for 4 people. Season both sides with salt and pepper. In medium to large skillet, melt 1 tablespoon of the butter over high heat. When bubbly, add onions and cook, stirring frequently, until soft. Push to the side of the skillet. Melt an additional 1 or 2 tablespoons of butter. When bubbly, add steaks and cook to medium-rare; depending upon the thickness and the heat from the fire, this should take 2 to 3 minutes on each side. Transfer steaks and onion to serving plates. Immediately melt remaining butter in skillet. Carefully crack each egg into skillet, keeping as separate as possible. Cook eggs to desired doneness; place next to the hot venison and onions.

Planning Ahead

☞ *Since breakfast at deer camp begins way before sunrise, it is to the cook's advantage to prep as many foodstuffs as possible the night before!*

☞ *If you plan to include some prepackaged food items such as bread mix or pudding mix in your camp menus, make sure to account for the additional ingredients needed to make them (eggs, oil, sugar, etc.) and add them to your packing list.*

LARGEMOUTH SCRAMBLE

As anyone who has ever fished the Pine Tree State knows, Maine is a paradise for both smallmouth and largemouth bass fishing, often providing more bass in a morning's outing than one could eat all week. One such morning, we caught our limit of bass from a coldwater creek that feeds some of Maine's pristine lakes. That night as I was making dinner, I cooked several extra bass for breakfast the next day (this is a tactic I often use to save time and effort in the morning). This recipe also works very well with salmon. A plate of hot biscuits makes a nice side.

<u>*Serves:*</u> 3 or 4
<u>*Cooking Time:*</u> Under 15 minutes

3 to 5 eggs	One-quarter of a small onion, chopped
1/4 cup milk	2 tablespoons butter
1 cup flaked leftover cooked largemouth bass	Salt and pepper
	1/4 cup shredded cheddar cheese

<u>*For Stovetop or Surface Cooking:*</u> In medium bowl, beat eggs gently with the milk. Add flaked fish and chopped onion. Mix thoroughly. In medium skillet, melt butter over medium heat. Add egg mixture and cook until set, stirring frequently. Season to taste with salt and pepper. Top portions with cheddar cheese.

BORDER-STYLE SCRAMBLED EGGS

I came across this recipe in 1984 while on a fabulous whitetail deer hunting trip in Texas. The chefs at camp were all Mexican, and for the entire week we ate the finest and most scrumptious zesty meals you could find north of the border. This recipe can be altered to suit preferences from hot to mildly spicy.

<u>*Serves:*</u> 2
<u>*Cooking Time:*</u> Under 15 minutes

2 flour tortillas	1 teaspoon vegetable oil
3 eggs	1 cup cubed leftover cooked venison
1/4 cup shredded cheddar cheese	1 avocado, diced
1 tablespoon milk	4 olives, pitted and minced
Tabasco sauce	1/4 to 1/2 cup salsa, warmed

<u>*For Stovetop or Surface Cooking:*</u> In skillet or Dutch oven, heat tortillas over medium heat until warm. Set aside in a covered dish or towel to keep warm. In mixing bowl, beat together the eggs, cheese, milk, and Tabasco sauce to taste; set aside. Add oil to same pan and heat over medium heat. Add venison and cook, stirring, until heated thoroughly. Add egg mixture. Cook until set, stirring frequently. Remove from heat and stir in avocado and olives. Spoon onto tortillas and roll up. Ladle warm salsa over each tortilla; serve immediately.

Smallmouth Stocking

☞ *Prior to 1900, smallmouth bass were found mainly in the Great Lakes and in river systems in the eastern United States. But as the railroads moved west and north, smallmouths were stocked in many rivers, natural lakes and large reservoirs. Probably the most successful introduction was in the clear, rocky lakes of southern Canada.*

BROOKIES 'N' BACON

One late spring morning, Peter and I were up early fishing for native brook trout in the pristine Adirondack mountain streams of New York State. Later that morning, when we arrived back at camp with a creel full of the tasty fish, I rustled up a batch of Brookies 'n' Bacon. Panfried eggs and potatoes rounded out the meal. Be sure to keep the trout cool until you cook them, as they spoil easily.

<u>Serves:</u> 3
<u>Cooking Time:</u> Under 15 minutes

6 slices bacon
$1/2$ cup all-purpose flour

$1/2$ cup cornmeal
6 whole small brook trout (about 4 ounces each), gutted and gilled

<u>For Stovetop or Surface Cooking:</u> In skillet, cook bacon over medium heat until crispy. While bacon is cooking, combine flour and cornmeal in dish or food-storage bag and coat trout with mixture. When bacon is done, remove from pan and set aside in a warm place. Add brookies to skillet with hot bacon grease; do not overcrowd skillet. If trout begin to curl up, flatten them with spatula to ensure they're cooked evenly throughout. Depending upon the intensity of the heat and the thickness of the trout, this should take 3 to 5 minutes. Test with a fork and when the flesh flakes easily, they are done. Serve trout with bacon.

SKEWERED SNAKE RIVER RAINBOW TROUT

Each time I write or talk about this recipe, my mouth waters. Freshly caught trout just doesn't get better than this. The combination of flavors will have you licking your chops until lunch!

<u>Serves:</u> 4
<u>Cooking Time:</u> Under 30 minutes

4 whole rainbow trout (8 oz. to 1 lb. each), gutted and gilled
Salt and pepper
1 onion, cut into 8 wedges

8 slices bacon
You will also need: Toothpicks, green sticks for grilling over the fire

<u>For Cooking Over Coals:</u> Prepare grill or campfire. Season insides of trout with salt and pepper; stuff with onion wedges. Wrap each trout with 2 slices of bacon and secure with toothpicks (or green twigs). Run green stick skewers through the mouth of the fish, under the backbone, and out through the tail.* Cook over an open flame, turning from time to time. Fish is done when the flesh flakes easily.

<u>For Camp or Home Cooking with a Broiler:</u> Season, stuff and wrap trout as directed above. Place under broiler for 3 to 5 minutes on each side, or until the flesh flakes easily.

*<u>Note:</u> If you have a hinged basket available, place the trout in the basket rather than skewering with sticks.

Winter Trout

☞ *As a general rule, the best winter trout fishing is where the stream is warmest. Trout often congregate around springs because groundwater is normally warmer than the surrounding water.*

☞ *Check snowy streambanks to determine if there is a midge hatch. Tiny dark insects resembling mosquitoes are probably midges; select a fly that resembles them. Drift a midge imitation just below the surface to catch feeding trout.*

QUAIL with EGGS

Quail is a magnificent and flavorful game bird, and it's not just for roasting. Try this recipe for breakfast . . . it's especially good served with fresh biscuits and hot coffee.

<u>*Serves:*</u> 2
<u>*Cooking Time:*</u> Under 30 minutes

Seasoned flour:
1 cup all-purpose flour
1 teaspoon garlic powder
   Salt and pepper to taste

3 slices bacon, chopped
4 to 6 dressed quail (4 to 8 oz. each), skin on
2 tablespoons oil, divided
4 to 6 wild onions, green parts chopped*
4 eggs, beaten

<u>*Optional Advance Preparation:*</u> Combine seasoned-flour ingredients in large plastic food-storage bag.

<u>*For Stovetop or Surface Cooking:*</u> In medium skillet or Dutch oven, cook bacon over medium heat until just crisp. Transfer to paper towel–lined plate and set aside. Discard drippings from skillet.

Shake quail in bag with seasoned flour, shaking off excess. Add 1 tablespoon of the oil to the skillet and heat over medium heat. Add floured quail to skillet and cook until golden brown on all sides. Transfer quail to dish; set aside and keep warm. Add onions to skillet, and sauté for 1 to 2 minutes. Add eggs and cooked bacon to skillet. Cook until eggs are set, stirring frequently. Divide eggs between 2 plates; top each with 2 or 3 quail.

<u>*Note:*</u> If you like, you may use both the white and green parts of the onion in this recipe; however, I like to use just the greens in this dish, saving the white parts for use in another dish.

Clever Quail

☞ *Bobwhite quail roost on the ground. During cool weather, they form a "roosting ring," huddling in a plate-sized circle with their tails pointed toward the center. This tactic preserves body heat.*

☞ *Besides the familiar "bob-bob-white" call, the birds make a "whoo-ee-whoo" rallying call to regroup a broken-up covey.*

KENAI RIVER SALMON FRITTATA

A frittata is a Mediterranean egg dish with all the ingredients mixed in during the cooking process — rather like a flat omelet. Here's a version that features leftover salmon or other fish, spiced up with onions and cheese.

Serves: 4
Cooking Time: Under 15 minutes

- 2 to 3 tablespoons vegetable oil
- 1 small onion, thinly sliced
- 8 button mushrooms, thinly sliced (or wild mushrooms, if you have them)
- 1 small tomato, seeded and chopped
-   Salt and pepper
- 6 eggs, beaten
- 1 cup flaked leftover cooked salmon
- 1/2 cup shredded Monterey Jack cheese

For Stovetop or Surface Cooking: Heat oil in large skillet or Dutch oven over medium heat. Add onion, mushrooms and tomato. Cook for about 3 minutes, stirring occasionally. Season with salt and pepper to taste. Add eggs and salmon. Stir to mix and then cook without stirring. When the first side is cooked (but not browned), flip and cook second side.* While second side is cooking, sprinkle cheese on top. When done, cut into 4 portions and serve warm.

*Note: If your frittata becomes too heavy to flip, lift the cooked egg mixture from the edges and tilt the pan to allow the runny egg mixture to flow underneath. Then, put a lid on the pan to help cook it from the top.

EL PIKE-O QUESADILLAS

A friend of ours shared this recipe with me while we were hunting caribou in Canada. Some of the hunters in the party shot their bulls early on in the trip, so they went fishing and came back with plenty of pike. I added the salsa to this recipe to help with the general dryness of pike, and it really enhances the flavor. Whether you use mild or spicy salsa, this is sure to be a camp favorite for anyone who enjoys Mexican-style eating.

Serves: 4
Cooking Time: Under 15 minutes

- 1 cup flaked leftover cooked pike
- 1 cup salsa
- 4 flour tortillas
- 1 cup shredded Monterey Jack or cheddar cheese
- 1/2 cup sour cream, optional

For Stovetop or Surface Cooking: In small bowl, mix cooked fish and salsa together. In medium skillet, heat 1 tortilla over medium heat for 1 to 2 minutes; do not allow it to brown. Flip tortilla over. While the second side is heating up, spoon one-quarter of the pike mixture over one half of the tortilla. Top pike mixture with one-quarter of the cheese. Fold the tortilla over on top of the cheese. Let it heat another minute or 2 (depending upon the flame). Set aside on a heated plate while you prepare remaining quesadillas, or serve immediately. If your camp has sour cream available, dollop a generous spoonful on top of the quesadilla before serving.

HEARTY ROCKY MOUNTAIN PANCAKES

The first time I made this recipe was in 1986 when we were camping in the Moose River flow of the Adirondack Mountains in New York. It was the last day of our trip, and I decided to make a dish that used all our leftovers. It turned out to be quite a favorite, and I've used it ever since.

Yield: 10 to 12 pancakes
Cooking Time: Under 30 minutes

1 cup pancake mix
1 cup cold water
1 teaspoon sugar
   Vegetable oil or shortening for frying
2 cups minced leftover cooked venison*
1 cup shredded cheddar cheese*

For Stovetop or Surface Cooking: In mixing bowl, combine pancake mix, water and sugar. Stir until mixture is smooth. Heat skillet over medium heat and add just enough oil or shortening to lightly coat the bottom. Pour about 2 tablespoons of batter into center of skillet and tilt skillet from side to side to spread batter out as thinly as possible. If you notice that the pancake is not spreading as much as you like, add a little more water, a teaspoon at a time, to thin out the batter. When first side is golden brown, flip pancake.

While second side is cooking, distribute 1 to 2 tablespoons minced venison and 1 tablespoon cheese over top of pancake. The cheese should melt slightly. When pancake is done, turn it out onto a plate, rolling it up as you turn it out; serve immediately.

*Note: For those not interested in early-morning venison, omit the meat and cheese. Instead, spread a little jelly on the pancake as the second side cooks and roll it up as you plate the pancake, just as with the venison ones.

Safety First

☞ *Regardless of whether you're hiking into the mountains or hunting on the prairie, you must plan for emergencies. For starters, always carry a first aid kit packed where it can be retrieved quickly, and learn how to use its contents. Second, always let a friend or family member know where you are going and when you plan to be out. Leave them a detailed map of where you'll park your vehicle and your planned route. Finally, be prepared with the proper clothing and gear for handling a drastic change in the weather.*

CREAMED PIKE over GRITS

Sometimes the best fishing for pike happens early in the season when it is still cold and damp. I usually reserve this recipe for that time of year — it's a rib-sticker that'll give you plenty of energy to fish any lake all day long.

Serves: 4
Cooking Time: Under 15 minutes

  4 cups water

For the creamed pike:
  2 tablespoons butter
  1 cup flaked leftover cooked pike
  1 tablespoon all-purpose flour
  1 tablespoon water
  1 cup milk
     Salt and pepper

For the grits:
  1 cup quick-cooking hominy grits
  1 teaspoon salt

For Stovetop or Surface Cooking: In medium saucepan, start water for the grits over high heat.* Meanwhile, melt butter in medium skillet over medium heat. Add pike and cook, stirring, until heated thoroughly. Transfer pike to a dish; set aside and keep warm. Add flour and 1 tablespoon water to the same skillet, stirring to make a smooth paste. Add milk, stirring constantly. Heat over medium heat for 1 to 2 minutes, stirring constantly. Return pike to skillet and simmer for about 3 minutes, stirring frequently. Remove from heat. Season to taste with salt and pepper; set aside and keep warm.

By now, the water for the grits should be boiling. Stir grits and salt into the boiling water. Cook for 3 to 5 minutes, stirring occasionally, until thick. Divide grits into 4 dishes; spoon the creamed pike over each portion.

*Note: If there is only one pan at camp, prepare the grits first, then set aside in a covered dish to help keep warm while you prepare the creamed pike.

Altitude

☞ *When camping and backpacking in the mountains, one must be aware of any drastic changes in altitude (above 6,000 feet or so) to avoid the possibility of falling victim to acute mountain sickness (AMS). The lower oxygen level also affects how one cooks at high elevations. The boiling point of water drops 9°F with every 5,000 feet in altitude. Because water boils at a lower temperature, the cooking time for foods doubles at 5,000 feet and quadruples at 10,000 feet. In addition, there are some stoves (such as alcohol stoves) that also cook more slowly than others at higher altitudes. Keep this in mind when planning your meals for the day.*

BUENO BURRITOS

This recipe was created on an elk hunting trip in Stonewall, Colorado. I was on a working cattle ranch where many of the hands were Mexican. I decided to rustle up some breakfast with a Mexican flare. The response was — bueno!

Rocky Mountain Elk Foundation

☞ *Since 1984, The RMEF has funded more than 2,700 conservation projects in 48 states and 8 Canadian provinces. In total, the RMEF has conserved and enhanced over 3,000,000 acres of wildlife habitat. For more information on how you can become a member, check them out at www.elkfoundation.org on the Internet. As a member, you'll get to enjoy the RMEF bi-monthly magazine, Bugle, which is packed with informative and entertaining articles.*

Serves: 4
Cooking Time: Under 15 minutes

    2 tablespoons vegetable oil
    4 flour tortillas
 1/4 cup water, approx.
 1/2 cup diced onion
 1/2 cup diced green bell pepper
 1/2 lb. leftover cooked venison roast, chopped
    4 eggs, beaten
 1/8 teaspoon chili powder
       Salt and pepper

For Stovetop or Surface Cooking: Preheat skillet or Dutch oven over medium heat. With your fingers, rub a little of the oil on both sides of the tortillas. Place about 1 tablespoon water in skillet; when it is hot, add 1 tortilla. Flip quickly to heat both sides. Place in foil near the heat to keep warm. Repeat with remaining tortillas, adding more water to skillet if needed. The purpose is to quickly warm the tortillas, not to cook them.

Heat remaining oil in skillet over medium-high heat. Add onion and pepper and sauté until softened. Add venison and cook, stirring, until heated thoroughly. Add eggs. Cook until set, stirring frequently. When almost done, season with chili powder, and salt and pepper to taste.

Unwrap the tortillas and fill each with one-quarter of the mixture. Fold up each, burrito-style. If you need to reheat, rewrap the finished burritos in foil. Place the package in the skillet; cover and heat over low heat for a few minutes.

BIGHORN RIVER FRITTERS

While taping a fly-fishing segment for our television series on the Bighorn River in 1988, the crew took a break and did some fishing. The next morning I had some leftover brown trout and created this easy-to-make and very scrumptious recipe.

<u>Serves:</u> 4
<u>Cooking Time:</u> Under 15 minutes

2 cups flaked leftover cooked trout
3 eggs, beaten
1 small onion, minced
1/4 cup all-purpose flour

1 tablespoon milk
Butter or vegetable oil for frying
Salt and pepper

<u>For Stovetop or Surface Cooking:</u> In mixing bowl, combine fish, eggs, onion, flour and milk; mix well. In medium skillet, heat enough butter or oil to come 1/4 inch up the sides of the skillet over high heat. Spoon fish mixture into skillet in 4 patties and cook until brown on both sides. Season to taste with salt and pepper before serving.

STREAMSIDE SALMON 'N' SPUDS

This is a streamside favorite of mine. On one of my first trips to Alaska I tried this recipe with each of the salmonids we caught during our trip. We were fishing during a peak year and, depending upon what section of the river we were fishing, we caught king, pink, coho, silver or chum salmon. I found the pink salmon to be the most delectable — but all provided a delicious and succulent streamside meal.

<u>Serves:</u> 3 or 4
<u>Cooking Time:</u> Under 30 minutes

1 lb. boneless salmon fillet, skin on
  Salt and pepper
2 tablespoons vegetable oil, divided

3 potatoes, cut into 1/4-inch dice
2 small onions, chopped
  Teriyaki sauce, optional

<u>For Stovetop or Surface Cooking:</u> Rub salmon fillet with salt and pepper to taste. Cut fillet into several pieces if the skillet you'll be cooking in is too small to accommodate it whole. Add 1 tablespoon of the oil to skillet and heat over medium-high heat. When oil is hot, add potatoes and onion. Cook until browned, stirring frequently. Push potatoes and onion to the side of the skillet. Place salmon in skillet, adding the additional 1 tablespoon oil if necessary. Reduce heat to medium and cook, turning from time to time, until fish flakes easily with a fork. If a small bottle of teriyaki sauce happened to find its way into your fishing vest early that morning, sprinkle a few drops on the salmon while it's cooking. Delicious!

Big Browns

☞ *Fly fishermen often bypass the lower stretches of rivers because the water is warmer, slower and usually muddier, but that may be a mistake. What looks like good carp water often holds the stream's biggest trout, particularly browns. Cast to them with large streamers, such as Wooly Buggers. Don't hesitate to use flies up to 4 inches in length.*

WALLEYE TACO SUPREME

A friend of ours has a cabin near the south shore of Lake Erie, a fishery known for an abundance of walleyes (especially in the spring). For many years, we had a friendly competition to see who would come up with the best recipe for walleye. This was my entry from a few years ago.

<u>*Serves:*</u> 4
<u>*Cooking Time:*</u> Under 15 minutes

	Juice from half of a lime
2	tablespoons vegetable oil
1	garlic clove, crushed, or 1 teaspoon garlic powder
1/2	teaspoon chili powder
1/2	teaspoon cumin
1/2	teaspoon crumbled dried oregano
4	walleye fillets (8 oz. each), boned but with skin on (white perch fillets will also work here)
	Salt and pepper
4	flour tortillas
2	medium tomatoes, seeded and chopped (or chop up a few canned tomatoes and gently squeeze out the excess juice)
1	avocado, diced (if available)
1	cup shredded cheddar cheese
	You will also need: Hinged grill basket or grill rack

For Cooking Over Coals: Prepare a grill or campfire. In small bowl or plastic bag, combine lime juice, oil, garlic, chili powder, cumin and oregano. Dip fillets in marinade to coat thoroughly. Place fillets on hinged grill basket or on grill rack, skin side down. Cook over medium-hot coals for 2 to 3 minutes, then turn and cook second side for 2 to 3 minutes longer. Remove from grill. Skin fillets and cut meat into bite-sized chunks; sprinkle with salt and pepper to taste. Heat tortillas over the coals until warm. Divide grilled fish chunks between tortillas. Top with equal portions of the tomatoes, avocado and cheese. Roll up tortillas and serve immediately.

For Camp or Home Cooking with a Broiler: Prepare as directed above, except cook fish under broiler for 3 to 4 minutes on each side.

Freshwater "Scallops"

☞ *Many anglers cut fillets off walleyes and discard the rest. They don't realize they're throwing away some of the best meat — the cheeks. They have a taste and texture very much like scallops.*

CREAMED TURKEY on TOAST

It was on a spring turkey hunt in Montana for Merriam's when I first experiment-ed with this recipe. I shot a gobbler in the morning and a few hours later, I was preparing this recipe in a one-room cattle shanty with only a stove, a table and a few chairs. The cowboys used this shack to prepare their meals when they were on the range. Our guide marveled at how easy this was to prepare and said he was going to use this recipe on special turkey hunts in the future.

<u>*Serves:*</u> 4
<u>*Cooking Time:*</u> Under 30 minutes

7/8 cup water, approx.
1/4 cup powdered milk
  3 tablespoons butter, divided
  1 lb. uncooked turkey breast, cubed
  2 cups fresh mushrooms, sliced
1/2 teaspoon Worcestershire sauce
     Salt and pepper
  2 tablespoons all-purpose flour
  4 pieces of thickly sliced bread

<u>*For Stovetop or Surface Cooking:*</u> Add enough water to the powdered milk to equal 1 cup; set aside. In skillet or Dutch oven, melt 1 tablespoon of the butter over high heat. When bubbly, add turkey cubes and mushrooms, stirring for a minute or so. Season with Worcestershire sauce, and salt and pepper to taste. Continue cooking until turkey is cooked through, 5 to 7 minutes. Remove from heat.

If you have 2 skillets, the sauce can be started at the same time. If not, transfer turkey to a warm dish, then wipe the first skillet clean and melt the remaining 2 tablespoons butter over low heat. Add flour and stir with wooden spoon until well blended. Let cook slowly for 5 to 7 minutes, but do not let it brown. Then slowly add the milk, stirring constantly. Continue cooking until the sauce thickens, stirring constantly. Season with salt and pepper to taste.

Add turkey mixture to sauce; stir to combine. Cook for about 5 minutes longer to combine flavors. Toast bread in clean skillet over the fire, or in hinged basket. Place 1 toasted slice of bread on each plate and pour creamed turkey on top.

Merriam's Wild Turkey

☞ *The Merriam's turkey, named in honor of the first chief of the United States Biological Survey, C. Hart Merriam, originally inhabited Arizona, New Mexico and Colorado, but stocking efforts have extended its range into the Dakotas, Montana, Nebraska, Oklahoma and the Pacific Northwest.*

☞ *The Merriam's rump feathers and tail tips are light buff to white, much lighter than those on the eastern turkey.*

BREAD
CAMP RECIPES

*T*here's something unique about baking a fresh loaf of bread. I enjoy hearing and seeing family member's reactions as they inhale the soothing aroma of the baking bread. It's also fun to watch their expressions as they break off a hot piece of bread, generously smear homemade jam all over it, and finally enjoy their first bite of this delicious treat. Their oohs, aahs and mmmmms let me know that crafting a loaf of homemade bread is time well spent.

I also enjoy watching folks as they dip biscuits into their over-medium eggs, lapping up the yolk; or use a thick slice of Skillet Bread still warm from the pan to clean up whatever scrumptious morsels are left on their plates.

Breads add flavor and substance to every meal. They're loaded with carbohydrates to supply much-needed energy throughout the day. A loaf of freshly baked bread, a pan of golden biscuits, or

a specialty like garlic bread will help make a good meal – great! This is especially true in camp, where even the simplest foods take on new flavors. Even some piping hot Bread-on-a-Stick – which is about as simple as it gets – will be immensely satisfying, especially when it's slathered with sweet butter.

These are just some of the reasons I always try to make bread of some sort when we are camping or when we are at our deer hunting cabin. The rich and tantalizing aromas from freshly made breadstuffs always seem to create a wonderful feeling of home – even when you're miles away from it.

Quick breads, biscuits or skillet bread are often easier to prepare at camp than regular yeast breads, which require lengthy rising times and controlled baking temperatures. However, if you have a leisurely camping schedule and will be around camp to attend to the dough periodically, traditional yeast bread is an unforgettable treat at camp.

Bread breaks down all inhibitions at a dinner table. People feel comfortable when bread is served, as it is an integral part of our social history. Bread completes each meal and and makes it more enjoyable. I consider bread to be the medium, the bridge that connects people to enjoying food and the company at any meal. So, the next time you're at camp, bake some Zesty Grilled Garlic Bread and it won't be long before you'll hear, "Pass another slice of bread, please!"

ZESTY GRILLED GARLIC BREAD

This is a real hit when there are bread and garlic lovers in camp. It stands alone as an appetizer, or makes a perfect side dish for a big plate of piping-hot pasta.

Serves: About 6 (depending on the size of the loaf)
Cooking Time: Under 15 minutes

Cheese mixture:

1/2 cup grated Parmesan cheese

1/2 teaspoon crumbled dried oregano

1/2 teaspoon paprika

1/4 cup mayonnaise or oil (preferably olive oil)

3 to 4 cloves garlic, minced

1 loaf French bread, sliced lengthwise

For cooking over coals you will also need: Grill grate or aluminum foil

Optional Advance Preparation: Combine cheese-mixture ingredients in plastic food-storage bag.

For Cooking Over Coals: Prepare grill or campfire. Add mayonnaise and garlic to bag with cheese mixture, or combine ingredients in small bowl; mix well. Spoon or pour mayonnaise mixture over both halves of the sliced bread.

If grill grate is available, place bread on grate, sliced side up; otherwise, place bread halves together, topped sides facing each other, and wrap in foil. Place over medium heat for 5 to 10 minutes, turning frequently. Do not let the bread burn.

For Camp or Home Cooking in an Oven: Heat oven to 350°F. Top bread as directed above and place on baking sheet, sliced side up. Bake for 10 minutes. Turn on broiler and place baking sheet under broiler. Broil until edges of bread are browned, about 3 minutes.

Prepping Foods

☞ *I always like to chop, slice or dice as many food items ahead of time as possible. Also, some canned items are available prechopped, like chopped mushrooms, sliced olives, etc. Any breading, seasoned flour or cake mix can be premixed at home, placed in a plastic resealable bag and labeled accordingly. In addition, dressings, marinades and sauces can also be mixed ahead of time and placed in plastic containers.*

BREAD-ON-A-STICK

If roasting marshmallows has become boring, then try this. It's a great alternative and lots of fun for all in the camp — both young and old.

Serves: 2
Cooking Time: Under 15 minutes

Flour mixture:

1 cup all-purpose flour
1 teaspoon baking powder
1/4 teaspoon salt

1 cup cold water

All-purpose flour for shaping dough (approx. 1/4 cup)

Butter and/or jam for serving

For cooking over coals you will also need: 1 or 2 green sticks about 1/2 inch in diameter.

Optional Advance Preparation: Combine flour-mixture ingredients in plastic food-storage bag.

For Cooking Over Coals: Prepare grill or campfire. Peel ends of the green sticks to remove bark. In mixing bowl, combine flour mixture and water; mix quickly until stiff dough is formed. (If you don't have a bowl handy, you can add the water to the bag with the flour mixture and knead it right in the bag.) With floured hands, flatten dough into 1 or 2 patties about 1/2 inch thick. Wrap around the end of a green stick and hold over hot coals. Turn frequently until cooked through. Slide off and serve hot with butter and/or jam.

For Camp or Home Cooking with a Broiler: Mix and roll as directed above, and cook under broiler. Since most broilers are usually placed high in the kitchen, this may be a bit difficult for youngsters to prepare.

WARM WILD BERRY JAM

If fresh berries are available near your camp, try this delectable and easy recipe. Serve over breads, warm pancakes, French toast or buttered toast ... fellow campers will beg for more!

Yield: 3 cups
Cooking Time: Under 15 minutes

4 cups wild berries (blueberries, strawberries, blackberries, or a mixture)
3 cups sugar
One-quarter of a lemon

For Stovetop or Surface Cooking: Combine berries and sugar in medium pot. Place over medium-high heat. Stir to mix sugar and berries together and then let be. Heat mixture to boiling. Squeeze lemon juice into the mixture and stir quickly. Remove from heat and set aside to cool.

Wild Berries

☞ *Blackberries and raspberries come from the same family (Rubus). Both plants feature clumps of berries, and each berry is composed of many seed-bearing sections. These berries ripen from early summer right through early fall. Since berries are a favorite of many birds, their seeds are widely distributed. You can find blackberry and raspberry bushes on the edges of farm fields or river banks, along logging roads and meadows, near swamps, and in the woods.*

Wild blueberries and huckleberries are almost

continued on page 27

CORN TORTILLAS

I like to make these when we are carrying only a limited amount of staples. They're delicious, healthy, and a great alternate for bread in the ol' PB&J staple.

continued from page 26

Yield: 8 to 10 tortillas

Cooking Time: 1¹/₂ hours

2 cups masa harina* (corn flour; available in large supermarkets or Mexican markets)

¹/₂ teaspoon salt

2 cups boiling water

You will also need: Waxed paper or tortilla press

For Stovetop or Surface Cooking: In medium bowl, stir together masa and salt. Make a well in the center and add about ¹/₂ cup of the boiling water. Mix well, and continue to add water, a little at a time, at first stirring with a spoon and then mixing with your hands (once the water has cooled enough) until dough is well mixed. It should be firm and springy rather than dry and crumbly. Cover and let stand for about 1 hour.*

Heat skillet or griddle over medium-high heat. Divide dough into 2-inch balls. Roll out a ball between 2 moistened pieces of waxed paper (a wine bottle or can of vegetables works well as a rolling pin), or flatten with a tortilla press; the tortillas should be very thin and even. Gently peel off one layer of waxed paper and place tortilla on hot skillet, paper side up. As tortilla heats up, peel off other layer of waxed paper. When first side is golden brown, flip tortilla and cook until golden brown on second side. Keep warm in a towel while you prepare remaining tortillas.

Note: If you are using instant masa, the dough does not have to stand for an hour; proceed with shaping immediately after mixing.

too similar to tell apart. Generally speaking, blueberries are larger and have a slight whitish hue to them, while huckleberries are smaller, darker and are a deeper blue/purple than blueberries. These berries ripen in the late summer. Blueberries and huckleberries need a lot of sunshine and usually are found on the edges of open fields, along logging roads, and in open brushy fields.

Always rinse berries under cool water to eliminate any insects, stems or leaves.

CHEDDAR BISCUITS

If your camp has an oven, this will be a favorite. If you don't have an oven, you can bake these using the classic Dutch oven technique, making sure that you preheat the lid and put enough coals on top of the lid for proper baking. There should be 6 to 8 coals underneath the Dutch oven (evenly spaced) and double that amount on top of the lid (also evenly spaced).

<u>Yield:</u> About 18 biscuits
<u>Cooking Time:</u> 30 to 60 minutes

Flour mixture:
2 1/2 cups all-purpose flour
1 1/2 teaspoons baking powder
1/2 teaspoon baking soda
1/2 teaspoon salt

5 tablespoons unsalted butter, cut into 1/2-inch pieces
1 cup shredded cheddar cheese
1 cup buttermilk or plain yogurt
1 egg
All-purpose flour for shaping dough (approx. 1/4 cup)
Butter for serving, optional
You will also need: Baking sheet (or Dutch oven and parchment paper)

<u>Optional Advance Preparation:</u> Combine flour-mixture ingredients in plastic food-storage bag.

<u>For Camp or Home Cooking in an Oven:</u> Heat oven to 450°F. In mixing bowl, combine flour mixture and unsalted butter. Using 2 knives, cut butter into flour until the mixture is crumbly. Stir in shredded cheese. In separate bowl, beat buttermilk and egg together until frothy. With a wooden spoon, stir buttermilk mixture into flour mixture to form a lumpy dough.

Lightly flour working surface and turn dough out onto it. Gently knead about 10 times and then roll dough out to a little less than 1/2 inch in thickness. With clean, sharp knife, cut dough into 2-inch squares and place on ungreased baking sheet. Bake for 10 to 12 minutes, until lightly browned. Remove from oven and serve warm with butter.

<u>For Dutch Oven Cooking:</u> For Dutch oven cooking: Prepare campfire; preheat Dutch oven lid in coals. Line bottom of Dutch oven with parchment paper cut to fit the bottom; this will prevent the biscuits from sticking. Arrange biscuits on parchment paper. Place preheated lid on Dutch oven. Position Dutch oven over small bed of coals; place additional hot coals on top of lid. Bake for 12 to 15 minutes.

Tips for Camping in Bear Country

☞ When camping in bear country, it is of the utmost importance to keep a campsite clean. That means washing all dishes and pots after every meal, putting all trash in closed plastic bags, and not leaving any food items sitting out in plain sight. Before going to bed at night or leaving camp for any period of time, hang the food and trash between two trees and high off the ground.

SKILLET BREAD

Bread is the mainstay for any camp or trailside meal. This is a traditional recipe for fried bread — seasoned with wild edibles!

<u>Yield:</u> 1 large bread "cake" (4 to 6 servings)
<u>Cooking Time:</u> Under 30 minutes

1/4	cup vegetable oil or shortening
21/4	cups buttermilk baking mix, divided
1/2	cup cold water
4	wild scallions, chopped

<u>For Stovetop or Surface Cooking:</u> Make sure your cooking fire has a steady low flame, whether it is a campfire or a stove. In skillet with at least an 8-inch-wide bottom, heat oil or melt shortening. In mixing bowl, stir together 2 cups of the baking mix, the water and scallions until mixture is well blended. Coat your hands with remaining baking mix, then pat dough into soft ball. Place dough into skillet and flatten, being careful not to burn your hands. Cook bread until it starts to brown on the bottom and begins to dry out. Be careful not to let the flames get too hot or the bread will burn. When first side is nicely browned, flip bread and cook until bread is browned on second side and no longer doughy in center.

Skillet Bread

☞ *Skillet bread is a staple of many camp meals — it's filling, uses easily packable ingredients, and is quick to make. Skillet bread was introduced in the Americas by European fur traders in the 18th century. Called bannock, from the Gaelic word for bread, it was an attempt to duplicate Scottish scones on a campfire. Nowadays there are many variations, but the basic recipe calls for flour, water, fat (traditionally, lard or bacon fat) and sometimes leavening. Preparation: In a large bowl, combine flour and fat until the mixture is crumbly. Add water until the dough is not sticky. Wrap the dough on a stick or fry in a heavy skillet over the campfire. The result is a hard, dry, portable bread.*

LIGHT MEALS & SIDES
CAMP RECIPES

One of the most colorful and striking fish is the American grayling – a little-known member of the Salmonid family. I was fishing the Upper Braids of the Alegnak River in Alaska the first time I caught one of these acrobatic, hard-fighting fish. The grayling has an unusually large dorsal fin with more than 17 rays, and the male's dorsal fin starts low and sweeps high up the back. Since they are shoreline feeders, they can often be spotted by the dimples created by their large dorsal fins as they cruise up and down riverbanks in search of worms and crustaceans. Grayling in these cold waters don't grow very fast, and one that weighs over 3 pounds is at least 7 years old.

Peter and I were casting terrestrials, mostly black ants and grasshoppers, when my first grayling hit. I recall that this fish hit just about as I was going to lift my line for a new cast. I heard a loud "WHAP" just as the grayling came out of the water and struck the grasshopper on his return to the river. I quickly set the hook and was exhilarated by the great fight I had with this energetic fish.

On this particular morning, we were lucky enough to hit a section of the river that provided nonstop action like this for several hours. Later, we returned to Tony Sarp's Katmai Lodge for lunch, where we were treated to an appetizer of fresh-smoked salmon made with the day's catch. There's nothing quite like eating fresh-caught fish or game you have just brought back to camp. The combination of fresh air, wildlife and the ambient sounds of nature make outdoor meals all that much more desirable.

This section of my cookbook includes some lighter meals and side dishes that you might enjoy preparing for lunch or a midday snack. In less than an hour you can serve up some of my delicious, piping hot Steelhead Chowder; serve a delectable side dish of Duck 'n' Dandelion Salad, or prepare a meal of tasty Salmon Croquettes. Any one of these recipes will delight your fellow outdoors enthusiasts. And to put the finishing touch on such culinary delights, may I suggest a chilled glass of Chardonnay?

LONG LAKE FISH CROSTINI

This side dish will wow your fellow campers — they won't expect such a tasty and interesting appetizer when trailside! I usually prepare this on the second or third day of a trip, when the bread is still fresh and there is leftover fish from a previous meal.

<u>Serves:</u> 2 or 3
<u>Cooking Time:</u> Under 15 minutes

6 slices French bread
2 tablespoons vegetable oil
2 cloves garlic, finely minced
   Salt and pepper
2 small tomatoes, thinly sliced

1½ cups flaked leftover baked or broiled fish
6 slices Swiss cheese
For cooking over coals you will also need: Aluminum foil, grill grate if available

For Cooking Over Coals: Prepare campfire or grill. Over a bed of hot coals, toast bread on both sides. In small bowl, mix oil, garlic, and salt and pepper to taste. Brush toasted bread on both sides with seasoned oil mixture. Place several tomato slices on each slice of bread. Top with about 1/4 cup of fish. Place slice of cheese on each crostini. Wrap well in foil.

If grill grate is available, place wrapped packets on grate, topped side up; otherwise, place wrapped packets on bed of cooler coals. Heat for about 5 minutes, just enough time to melt the cheese.

For Camp or Home Cooking with a Broiler: Toast bread under broiler until just browned, about 2 minutes. Assemble crostini as directed, but do not wrap in foil. Place assembled crostini under broiler until cheese melts.

SALMON CROQUETTES

Although I like to make these tasty tidbits as a lunch meal in camp or at the cabin, they make delightful holiday starters as well.

<u>Serves:</u> 2 or 3
<u>Cooking Time:</u> Under 15 minutes

2 eggs
2 cups flaked leftover cooked salmon
1 tablespoon minced parsley
1 tablespoon finely chopped onion

1 cup crushed cracker crumbs or breadcrumbs
1/4 cup vegetable oil, approx.

For Stovetop or Surface Cooking: In mixing bowl, lightly beat the eggs. Add salmon, parsley and onion, and mix gently but thoroughly. Form into cylindrical croquettes. Roll in cracker crumbs to coat entirely. Heat about 1/4 inch of cooking oil in large skillet or Dutch oven over medium-high heat. Panfry croquettes for 3 to 5 minutes, until evenly browned on all sides. Serve warm.

Foil Around the Fire!

☞ Foil can also be used as a reflector when you want to retain some of the heat generated by a campfire. Try to prevent the foil reflector from getting sooty, as it is the shiny part of the foil that does the reflecting!

☞ To make a foil windscreen for your fire, you'll need at least 2 pieces of heavy-duty aluminum foil, each about 2 to 3 feet long. Put the 2 pieces together and make a 2- to 3-inch rim at the bottom. Fold the screen around the fire site and secure on the ground with some smaller rocks. If the materials aren't handy for one, then pile up rocks on the windy side of the fire to help break the wind.

CORN-ROW PHEASANT GRILLED PIZZA

Preparing this recipe is almost as much fun as hunting for the pheasant itself. Pheasant is among the tastiest of all wild game birds and this recipe really enhances its flavor.

Serves: 2
Cooking Time: Under 30 minutes

3/4 lb. pheasant breast meat, cut into
    1/2-inch chunks
1/4 teaspoon cayenne pepper
1/4 teaspoon black pepper
1/8 teaspoon salt
3 tablespoons vegetable oil, divided
1 medium onion, sliced
1 bell pepper (any color), cored and diced

2 cloves garlic, minced
1 1/4 cups Easy Camp Tomato Sauce (page 48)
    Cornmeal for dusting
4 large flour tortillas
1 cup shredded Monterey Jack cheese
1/2 teaspoon crumbled dried oregano
    You will also need: Basting brush; grill grate
    (or ridged grill pan for stovetop cooking)

For Cooking Over Coals: Prepare campfire or grill; place grate over coals. Since grilled pizzas cook very quickly, it's essential that you have all your toppings ready to go before you begin grilling.

Season the pheasant chunks with cayenne pepper, black pepper and salt. Heat 1 tablespoon of the oil in a skillet over medium-high heat. Toss in the pheasant chunks and stir-fry until they are cooked through. Transfer to a bowl. Add another tablespoon of the oil to the skillet. When hot, toss in the onion and bell pepper and stir-fry for about 3 minutes, or until tender-crisp. Add garlic and continue stir-frying until garlic is golden. Add tomato sauce and mix thoroughly. Remove from heat.

Sprinkle work surface lightly with cornmeal. Lightly brush 1 side of 2 of the flour tortillas with some of the remaining oil. Flip tortillas over onto cornmeal. In this way, the cornmeal will adhere to the oiled side of the tortillas. Place the 2 tortillas on grill grate with the cornmeal side down. Lightly oil the top side of the tortillas on the grate, then place another tortilla on top of the ones on the grill and oil the tops lightly. Each "pizza crust" will now consist of 2 stacked tortillas. Transfer crusts to a cooler part of the grill.

Quickly top the crusts with half of the tomato sauce mixture. Divide the stir-fried pheasant bits and shredded cheese between the 2 crusts, and sprinkle each with half of the oregano. Cover grill and cook for 2 to 3 minutes, or until cheese begins to melt. Remove from grill and serve immediately.

For Stovetop or Surface Cooking: Prepare pheasant and sauce mixtures as directed above. Heat a ridged grill pan over high heat until hot. Oil 2 tortillas and dust with cornmeal as directed above; set aside. Place 1 of the plain tortillas in the heated grill pan, and warm on both sides. Remove from pan. Add a cornmeal-coated tortilla to pan, cornmeal side up, and heat briefly. Turn carefully so the cornmeal side is down; top with the plain, heated tortilla. Add half of the tomato sauce mixture, pheasant and cheese; sprinkle with half of the oregano. Cover partially and cook until the cheese melts. Or, if you prefer, place the whole skillet under the broiler for the final cooking stage and broil until cheese melts. Repeat with remaining ingredients.

PHEASANT NIBBLES

One of our first bird dogs was named Stonegate, after the pheasant preserve that gave her to Peter. Stoney loved to hunt pheasant and was a regular on our television series. She was the perfect guest: she answered all calls/questions, was spontaneous in front of the camera and always seemed to have a smile on her face even when the weather wasn't the best. And, as with most labs, her energy seemed endless in the field as she did an excellent job in bringing home pheasants for the table. Here's a recipe that we first enjoyed during a midmorning break from hunting with Stoney. For us, it always hits the spot!

Serves: 2
Cooking Time: Under 15 minutes

1 boneless, skinless pheasant breast, cut into bite-sized chunks
1/4 cup all-purpose flour
1/4 cup butter (half of a stick), divided

Salt and pepper
1 teaspoon minced garlic chives
1 lemon

For Stovetop or Surface Cooking: Toss pheasant chunks in the flour, shaking off excess. In small skillet, heat half of the butter over medium-high heat until melted; do not let the butter brown. Add pheasant chunks and cook no longer than 3 to 5 minutes. Remove pheasant from skillet; season with salt and pepper. Melt remaining butter in same skillet over a low flame. Add garlic chives. Squeeze the juice from the lemon into skillet (there should be 3 or 4 tablespoons); stir well. Transfer lemon sauce to a small bowl. Serve the pheasant nibbles with toothpicks and the lemon sauce.

WILD CHANTERELLE MUSHROOM TOAST POINTS

This is a nice appetizer that's delicious and dainty. Chanterelles are readily available throughout much of the country in the wild or you can bring some along. It's a top choice in our camp.

Serves: 2
Cooking Time: Under 15 minutes

1 cup finely chopped fresh chanterelle mushrooms
1/4 cup finely chopped wild onion
3 tablespoons butter
3 tablespoons heavy cream, room temperature

Dash of garlic salt
Freshly ground pepper
2 slices bread, toasted and cut into quarters

For Stovetop or Surface Cooking: In medium skillet, sauté mushrooms and onion in butter until tender, about 5 minutes. Remove skillet from heat to let temperature drop slightly. Stir in cream, and season with garlic salt and pepper. Stir over low heat for about 3 minutes. Spoon over toast points and serve immediately.

Wild Mushrooms

☞ *Wild mushrooms are a succulent addition to many dishes, and can even serve as the focal point of a meal. But even if you are very experienced in wild mushroom hunting, always proceed with caution. I recommend reading mushroom ID books, as they will help greatly in properly identifying the good ones from the bad.*

FISH CAKE SUPREME

With quick and easy recipes like this that use leftover cooked fish, it doesn't matter if your previous meal of baked lake trout, grilled salmon or walleye was more than you and your fellow campers could eat. This makes for tasty lunch fare.

<u>Yield:</u> 8 fish cakes
<u>Cooking Time:</u> Under 15 minutes

1 egg	1 teaspoon minced onion
1 cup flaked leftover cooked fish	1/4 teaspoon salt
1 cup mashed potatoes (prepared instant will work fine)	1 cup crushed cracker crumbs, such as Saltines or Ritz
2 tablespoons all-purpose flour	1/4 cup vegetable oil, approx.
1 teaspoon lemon juice	

For Stovetop or Surface Cooking: In mixing bowl, lightly beat the egg. Add fish, potatoes, flour, lemon juice, onion and salt; mix gently but thoroughly. Form into round cakes. Roll in cracker crumbs to coat entirely. Heat about 1/4 inch of cooking oil in large skillet or Dutch oven over medium-high heat. Panfry fish cakes for 3 to 5 minutes, until evenly browned on both sides. Serve warm.

EGG SALAD DELUXE

This is a mainstay in any camp — lean-to, tent or cabin. Eggs are always a camp food staple, and the bacon adds a special flavor to otherwise common table fare.

<u>Serves:</u> 4
<u>Cooking Time:</u> Under 30 minutes

6 eggs	1 teaspoon snipped chives
1 quart water, approx.	1/2 teaspoon dry mustard
2 tablespoons mayonnaise	1/8 teaspoon paprika
1 tablespoon diced celery	Dash of Worcestershire sauce
1 tablespoon minced onion	Salt and pepper
1 tablespoon cooked, crumbled bacon or imitation bacon-flavored bits	2 pocket-style pita breads

For Stovetop or Surface Cooking: In saucepan, boil eggs in water to cover generously for 7 to 10 minutes. Plunge into cold water to stop cooking and to cool. While eggs are cooling, combine mayonnaise, celery, onion, bacon, chives, mustard and paprika in a mixing bowl; stir to combine. Add Worcestershire sauce, and salt and pepper to taste. Peel cooled eggs. Chop and add to mixing bowl; mix well. Cut pita breads into quarters and stuff with filling.

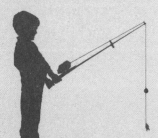

Fishing with Kids

☞ *Whenever you take a kid fishing, remember that the name of the game is "action!" Concentrate on sunfish, perch, rock bass or other species that you know are abundant and easy to catch. Use these times to teach kids the proper way to feel for a strike, set the hook, and fight a fish. Most of all, make it fun. If they lose interest after only an hour or so, simply pack up and leave the water with a smile. Chances are good that next time they'll want to stay longer. And if all goes well, it won't take too many fishing trips and you'll be the one asking to call it a day.*

CATFISH HOAGIES

Catfish, with its homely appearance, is often neglected by anglers. It's too bad, because the catfish is a good fighter, and its flesh is among the most delicate and tasty of all freshwater fish. This recipe featuring catfish is a real winner.

Serves: 4
Cooking Time: Under 15 minutes

  4 boneless, skinless catfish fillets (4 oz. each)
  2 tablespoons lemon juice
1/4 teaspoon pepper
1/8 teaspoon salt
    Vegetable oil for brushing grill basket
  3 tablespoons mayonnaise
  1 tablespoon honey-mustard dressing
  4 hoagy rolls, split
  1 medium tomato, sliced
    For cooking over coals you will also need: Hinged grill basket

For Cooking Over Coals: Prepare grill or campfire. Brush catfish fillets with lemon juice. Sprinkle both sides with pepper and salt. Brush grill basket with oil; place fish into grill basket. Cook over medium-hot coals for about 4 minutes on each side, or until fish flakes easily with fork.

Meanwhile, stir together mayonnaise and honey-mustard dressing in small bowl; spread on rolls. When fish is cooked, top each roll with 1 fillet. Divide tomato slices evenly between hoagies. Serve immediately.

For Camp or Home Cooking with a Broiler: Preheat broiler and broiler pan. Prepare fillets as directed above. Place fillets on hot broiler pan. Place pan 3 inches from broiling unit. Broil for 3 to 4 minutes on each side, or until flesh flakes easily with a fork.

Surface Cooking Over a Campfire

☞ *A campfire grate makes it easier to manage a pot or skillet without fear of it tipping over, and also allows you to move it to a hotter or cooler area of the coals as necessary. The outside of the cookware will be covered with soot after cooking; to make cleanup easier, rub it with liquid dish soap before placing it over the fire, and the soot will wash off easily afterward.*

STEELHEAD CHOWDER

I've been fishing for steelhead for nearly 20 years, mostly along the Salmon River in Pulaski, New York. My best successes have come while fishing from a drift boat using pink hot shots, or from the shoreline drifting salmon eggs. Although winter fishing can sometimes be uncomfortable, the effort is well worthwhile. On every successful trip, I keep at least one good-sized steelie to take home.

<u>Serves:</u> 8
<u>Cooking Time:</u> 30 to 60 minutes

    5 or 6 white potatoes, washed and cut into 1/2-inch chunks
    3 medium onions, chopped
    1 quart water, more if needed
 1/2 cup butter (1 stick)
    1 can (13 oz.) evaporated milk
    2 lbs. boneless, skinless steelhead, cut into bite-sized chunks
       Salt and pepper

For Stovetop or Surface Cooking: In Dutch oven, combine potatoes and onions. Add water to cover. Heat to boiling over high heat. Cook for 25 to 30 minutes. Add butter and evaporated milk; stir to mix well. Let simmer for about 10 minutes. Add fish chunks and stir to mix well. Simmer for about 10 minutes, or until fish flakes easily. Season with salt and pepper to taste. Serve hot.

CHEESY CORN CHOWDER

This rib-sticking dish is perfect for fall or winter camp. It'll keep you going all day whether you are hunting, snowmobiling, cross-country skiing or just hiking.

<u>Serves:</u> 4
<u>Cooking Time:</u> Under 30 minutes

    1 cup diced cooked potatoes
    1 cup whole-kernel corn, drained if canned
    1 can (14 1/2 oz.) chicken broth
    2 cups milk, divided
 1/3 cup all-purpose flour
 1/8 teaspoon pepper
    1 cup shredded cheddar cheese

For Stovetop or Surface Cooking: In soup pot, combine cooked potatoes, corn and chicken broth; place over medium heat. In small bowl, combine 2/3 cup of the milk with the flour and pepper. Mix with whisk or fork until thoroughly combined. Stir milk mixture into soup pot, along with remaining milk. Heat to a gentle boil, stirring occasionally. Continue cooking until the soup is as thick as you like it, then add cheese. Cook over low heat until cheese melts.

Adding Flavor to Canned Foods

☞ *If you are using canned and freeze-dried food items, use herbs and spices to give them a better taste. The spices and herbs that I always carry include: salt, pepper, garlic powder, cayenne, dried oregano, dried basil leaves, ground cinnamon, ground nutmeg, chili powder, curry powder, sesame seeds and crushed red pepper flakes. I recommend placing herbs and spices in leftover film containers, which are smaller than most containers from the camping store (and cheaper!). Remember to label the tops of the containers accordingly. Leftover prescription bottles from the pharmacy work well for storing slightly larger quantities of dry goods such as a cinnamon-sugar mix or Cajun spice blend.*

SALMON SOUP

Although I have fished for salmon in the Midwest, Alaska and Washington, most of my salmon fishing has been done in Niagara County, New York. Bill Hilts Jr., the sportfishing coordinator for Niagara County, has graciously hosted us several times for our television show. Each time, we have caught enough salmon from the lakes and rivers of the area to last throughout the year. Because we have so much salmon in the freezer, I've enjoyed coming up with many ways to prepare this tasty fish. Here is one of the recipes I use when camping. It's good served with skillet bread and butter.

Serves: 4
Cooking Time: 30 to 60 minutes

  4 potatoes, diced
1 1/2 quarts water
  1 lb. boneless, skinless salmon, cut into bite-sized chunks
  2 teaspoons salt
1/8 teaspoon pepper

For Stovetop or Surface Cooking: In Dutch oven, simmer potatoes in water for 40 minutes. Add remaining ingredients and let cook for about 10 minutes longer.

GOBBLER SOUP

While chicken soup seems to be the cure-all at home, I recommend wild turkey soup to warm up bodies and stave off sniffles while on the trail. This recipe can also be prepared with other cooked wild game birds like grouse, chukar and pheasant.

Serves: 4
Cooking Time: 30 to 60 minutes

  3 cups water
  2 cups cooked wild turkey breast, cut into bite-sized chunks before measuring
  2 red-skinned potatoes, chopped
  1 carrot, chopped
  1 medium onion, chopped
  3 chicken bouillon cubes
  1 clove garlic, crushed
1/4 teaspoon cayenne pepper
    Salt and pepper
  1 small tomato, quartered and seeded
1/2 cup canned or cooked kidney or black beans, drained if canned
    All-purpose flour (to thicken soup if necessary)

For Stovetop or Surface Cooking: In Dutch oven, heat water to boiling over high heat. Add turkey, potatoes, carrot, onion, bouillon cubes, garlic, cayenne, and salt and pepper to taste. Return to boiling, stirring occasionally. Cover and reduce heat. Simmer for about 30 minutes. Add tomato and beans. Re-cover and simmer for about 15 minutes longer. Thicken with flour if necessary.

The Grand Slam

☞ *If you hang around turkey hunters enough, eventually you'll hear one of them talk about "the grand slam." Did they suddenly change the subject to baseball? No. In hunter lingo, the turkey grand slam is achieved when you shoot each of the four major subspecies: the eastern, Merriam's, Rio Grande and Florida wild turkeys. Adding the Gould's is called the royal slam, and a hunter who adds the sixth subspecies, the Ocellated, has earned a world slam.*

GROUSE 'N' PEA SOUP

I find that grouse is one of the better game birds to eat as leftovers — although it's rare that we have a lot left over! When it does happen, I like to make this simple pick-me-up.

Serves: 2
Cooking Time: 30 to 60 minutes

2 1/2 cups water
1/4 teaspoon salt
1 cup freeze-dried green peas
1/2 cup cooked grouse breast, cut into 1/2-inch chunks before measuring
2 slices bacon, cooked and crumbled
1 carrot, diced
1/2 teaspoon crumbled dried marjoram

For Stovetop or Surface Cooking: In soup pot or small Dutch oven, combine water and salt. Heat to boiling over high heat. Add remaining ingredients and mix well. Cover and reduce heat; simmer for about 45 minutes, or until peas and carrot are tender, stirring occasionally.

ORIENTAL PHEASANT NOODLE SOUP

This is a favorite camp recipe, especially on our special pheasant hunting trips to Montana. Our rented cabin has few amenities, and cooking is always an adventure. This recipe is quick and easy to prepare and always sticks to the ribs, providing lots of energy for hunting on the cold and windy Montana prairie lands.

Serves: 2 or 3
Cooking Time: Under 15 minutes

4 cups water
2 packages (3 oz. each) Oriental-flavor Ramen noodle soup
1 1/2 cups cooked pheasant, cut into bite-sized chunks before measuring
2 tablespoons tomato paste

For Stovetop or Surface Cooking: In saucepan, heat water to boiling over high heat. Add soup noodles. Cook, stirring constantly, for about 2 minutes. Add pheasant chunks and tomato paste. Stir until tomato paste is dissolved. Remove from heat and stir in 1 to 1 1/2 of the seasoning packets from the soup. Mix well. Serve immediately.

Note: The noodles can be prepared ahead if necessary. But, because these particular noodles are so fine, they can get mushy when prepped and cooled. Since the noodles cook so quickly — within 2 minutes — I advise cooking these on the trail rather than in advance.

Foul-Weather Pheasants

☞ *In cold and windy weather, look for ring-necked pheasants in the tallest, thickest cover available. Trees or tall weeds offer better shelter for the birds than the surrounding lower cover.*

☞ *In the late season, once ponds have at least 4 inches of ice, hunt for pheasants in wetlands such as cattail swamps. When crops are harvested and grassy cover gets matted down by snow, wetlands may be the only cover remaining.*

TURKEY <u>and</u> RICE SOUP

During a normal year, I get to hunt wild turkeys in three or four states, often in remote locations. I came up with this recipe while hunting Rio Grandes from a motorhome in Texas. Its simplicity is surpassed only by its flavor.

<u>*Serves:*</u> 3 or 4
<u>*Cooking Time:*</u> Under 15 minutes

  1 can (14^1/$_2$ oz.) chicken broth
1^1/$_2$ cups instant rice
 ^{3}/$_4$ lb. cubed cooked turkey (about 2 cups of bite-sized chunks)
  1 can (10^3/$_4$ oz.) condensed cream of chicken soup
  1 cup milk (or half milk/half water), approx.

<u>*For Stovetop or Surface Cooking:*</u> In saucepan, combine chicken broth and instant rice. Cook over high heat for 3 to 5 minutes. Add turkey, cream of chicken soup, and a soup can of milk or milk/water mixture. Stir well and heat for an additional 3 to 5 minutes.

WILD RICE <u>and</u> DUCK SOUP

If your waterfowl hunting goes along the same line as mine does, you'll find yourself in a small, rustic cabin keeping the fire warm and coming up with another way to cook duck. This one always seems to be a favorite.

<u>*Serves:*</u> 4
<u>*Cooking Time:*</u> 30 to 60 minutes

  2 tablespoons butter
  1 carrot, sliced
  1 stalk celery, sliced
^{1}/$_2$ lb. fresh wild mushrooms, sliced (canned mushrooms, drained, will also work)
^{1}/$_2$ cup uncooked wild rice
  1 quart chicken broth
  1 cup chopped cooked duck meat
^{1}/$_2$ cup heavy cream, room temperature (if not available, substitute ^{3}/$_8$ cup milk and 2^1/$_2$ tablespoons butter)
    Salt and pepper

<u>*For Stovetop or Surface Cooking:*</u> In Dutch oven, melt butter over medium-high heat. Add carrots and celery. Sauté for a minute or so, then cover and cook for about 5 minutes. Add mushrooms, wild rice and chicken broth. Cover and cook for 45 minutes, or until rice is tender, stirring occasionally. Stir in duck meat and heavy cream; mix thoroughly. Cook for 5 to 10 minutes longer. Season with salt and pepper to taste.

Fooling Late-Spring Turkeys

☞ *If you pursue wild turkeys in the late spring, your best strategy is to hunt open fields with decoys and keep your calling to a minimum. Because the forest is thick with new green growth, the gobblers must use open fields to strut their stuff and be noticed by hens. In addition, because the birds have been hunted for several weeks, they are often call-shy. To be successful, simply set up in a known open-field strutting zone, and place a hen decoy about 20 yards out from your location. Place a jake decoy near the hen at 18 yards. Call enough to elicit a single gobble response from a tom, then shut up and wait for him to arrive. Your patience will pay off.*

CHICKEN CHOWDER

As many grandmothers have said, chicken soup will cure whatever ails you. Here's a variation of chicken soup that Grandma would approve of — and you don't even have to be sick to enjoy it.

<u>Serves:</u> 4
<u>Cooking Time:</u> Under 15 minutes

  1 medium carrot, thinly sliced
  1 cup whole-kernel corn, drained if canned
  1/2 cup peeled, shredded potato
  1/2 cup water
  1/4 cup chopped onion
  2 cups milk
  1 1/2 cups diced cooked chicken (pheasant, turkey or grouse will work, too)
  1 can (10 3/4 oz.) condensed cream of chicken soup
    Salt and pepper

<u>*For Stovetop or Surface Cooking:*</u> In soup pot, combine carrot, corn, potato, water and onion. Heat to boiling over high heat. Reduce heat and simmer for 5 to 7 minutes, stirring occasionally. Stir in milk, chicken and condensed soup. Cook for 2 to 3 minutes longer or until heated through, stirring occasionally. Season with salt and pepper to taste. Serve hot.

PESTO PASTA SOUP

As a dedicated Seinfeld fan, I love the episode where George can't figure out why he orders pesto every time he eats out — even though he hates it. (Each time he orders it, he thinks he'll grow to like it.) Pesto isn't for everyone. But if you are a pesto lover, you'll love this recipe.

<u>Serves:</u> 3
<u>Cooking Time:</u> Under 30 minutes

  2 cloves garlic, minced
  1 tablespoon vegetable oil
  2 cans (14 1/2 oz. each) chicken broth
  1/2 cup uncooked small macaroni such as ditalini

  1 carrot, diced
  1/2 cup sliced celery
  2 cups spinach (drained if canned), chopped
  3 tablespoons prepared pesto

<u>*For Stovetop or Surface Cooking:*</u> In soup pot, cook garlic in oil over high heat until golden brown (but don't burn it). Quickly add chicken broth and macaroni. Heat to boiling and cook for about 7 minutes, stirring occasionally. Add carrot, celery and spinach. Cook for 3 to 5 minutes longer, stirring occasionally. Divide among serving bowls. Drizzle 1 tablespoon pesto into each bowl. Eat hot!

Sleeping under the Stars

☞ *By taking the proper precautions you can stay dry in a tent regardless of how hard it rains. First, look for a piece of ground with a gentle slope. Remove any rocks, branches and pine cones that will make sleeping uncomfortable. Next, fold a plastic tarp to the size of your tent floor. Fold the excess under the tarp so any rain water that trickles down the slope doesn't pool on top of the tarp. Finally, place your tent on top of the tarp. Make sure that no part of the tarp is exposed. For comfort, sleep with your head on the high side of the slope.*

RAINY DAY VENISON CHILI

During hunting season, nothing is more loved by campers or cabin dwellers than a bowl of hot, steaming chili. You can't go wrong with this one.

<u>*Serves:*</u> 4
<u>*Cooking Time:*</u> Over 1 hour

- 4 slices bacon, chopped
- 1 cup chopped onion
- 1/4 cup chopped green bell pepper
- 1 lb. venison, cut into 1/2- to 1-inch cubes
- 1 can (15 oz.) kidney beans, drained
- 1 can (11 oz.) whole-kernel corn, drained
- 1 cup chopped fresh or canned tomatoes (if canned, drain before chopping)
- 1 cup chopped mushrooms (fresh or canned)
- 1 cup water
- 2 teaspoons chili powder
- 1 teaspoon cumin
- 1/2 teaspoon salt
- 3 cloves garlic, minced
- 1/4 cup all-purpose flour, approx.

<u>*For Stovetop or Surface Cooking:*</u> In Dutch oven, cook bacon over medium heat until just crisp, stirring occasionally. Add onion and green pepper to Dutch oven; cook until tender, stirring occasionally. Remove bacon and vegetables from Dutch oven, leaving drippings in pan; set aside. Add venison to Dutch oven and cook until meat is browned on all sides, stirring occasionally. While venison is cooking, in mixing bowl combine remaining ingredients except flour; stir well to combine. When venison is browned, return bacon and vegetables to Dutch oven. Add mixture from mixing bowl and stir well to mix thoroughly. Cover and reduce heat. Simmer for 45 minutes to 1 hour. Near the end of cooking time, sprinkle a little flour in to thicken the chili; stir well and continue cooking until thickened as desired.

DUCK 'N' DANDELION SALAD

The next time you're looking for something that's different, try this delicious and refreshing salad.

<u>*Serves:*</u> 4
<u>*Preparation Time:*</u> Under 15 minutes

- 4 cups dandelion greens, well washed
- 3/4 cup cooked duck meat, cut into bite-sized chunks before measuring
- Half of a medium onion, sliced
- 1 cup blue cheese dressing*
- Salt and pepper

<u>*No Cooking Required:*</u> Wash dandelion greens thoroughly to rid them of any natural pests and dirt. Pat dry with paper towels. Tear greens into bite-sized pieces and combine them with duck meat, onion and blue cheese dressing in mixing bowl. Toss gently, adding salt and pepper to taste.

*If blue cheese dressing isn't available, any oil-and-vinegar-based dressing will also work well.

Dandelion Greens

☞ *These plants grow wild in fields almost everywhere. (Look for remote areas that have not been treated with any pesticides.) Although they grow from spring through fall, dandelion leaves are best when harvested in early spring before the yellow flowers bloom. They have a slightly bitter taste but are enjoyed at many camps as well as in fine restaurants.*

PIKE'S PETE SALAD

Whenever we fish for pike in Canada, I make this recipe. When I was trying to name this recipe, our French guide suggested this one. When we asked him why he was suggesting "Pikes Peak," he replied, "Because Peter has so much fun fishing for them." It was then that I realized that he really was saying "Pike's Pete." When preparing this in Canada, you could change the name to Pike's Pierre Salad.

Serves: 4 to 6
Preparation Time: Under 15 minutes

2 lbs. cooked pike, flaked	1 tablespoon mayonnaise
1/4 cup vegetable oil	Salt and pepper
2 tablespoons vinegar	Crackers or bread for serving
2 cups chopped celery	

No Cooking Required: Place fish in mixing bowl. In a small bowl, mix oil and vinegar together. Pour over fish. Add celery and mayonnaise, and stir to combine. Season with salt and pepper to taste. Serve on crackers or bread.

CATFISH RICE SALAD

Here's a good way to use leftover catfish. You'll see how well the texture and flavor of catfish work with rice when you try this recipe.

Serves: 4
Cooking Time: 30 to 60 minutes

6 slices bacon, chopped
1 medium onion, chopped
1/4 cup chopped green bell pepper
2 cups diced tomatoes (or 1-lb. can, drained)
2 cups water
1 cup white rice
1/4 cup ketchup
1 teaspoon salt
1/4 teaspoon pepper
1 1/2 cups cooked catfish, in bite-sized pieces

For Stovetop or Surface Cooking: In Dutch oven or deep skillet, cook bacon over medium heat until crisp. Remove from skillet and set aside. Discard all but 3 tablespoons bacon drippings. Return Dutch oven to heat and fry the onion and green pepper until soft. Add cooked bacon, tomatoes, water, rice, ketchup, salt and pepper to Dutch oven. Cover and reduce heat; simmer for about 20 minutes. Check the consistency; the water should be almost completely absorbed. Add fish and stir to combine thoroughly. Cook for 5 to 10 minutes longer. Serve hot.

Catching Trophy Pike

☞ Many anglers use lures and live baits that are too small to get the attention of big northern pike. Believe it or not, adult pike (and muskies) will eat fish from one-fourth to one-half of their own length, and up to 20 percent of their own weight. Here's a simple formula to remember the next time you're after giant pike: Big Lures = Big Fish!

☞ Remember that little fish taste better than big fish. If you're lucky enough to land a trophy pike, let it go. Keep the 2- to 5-pounders for mealtime.

FISH <u>and</u> CORN SALAD

When summer vegetables are at their peak, simple dishes are often the best choice. It doesn't get much simpler than this easy recipe! But I promise you'll remember its flavor for a long time to come.

Serves: 4
Preparation Time: Under 15 minutes

- 1 to 1¹/₂ lbs. broiled or baked fish, skin and bones removed
- 2 cans (14¹/₂ oz. each) whole-kernel corn, drained, or about 3 cups cooked corn kernels
- Half of a small onion, chopped
- 1 cup chopped zucchini
- ¹/₂ cup chopped green bell pepper
- ¹/₂ cup vinaigrette dressing
- ¹/₄ teaspoon paprika

No Cooking Required: Cut fish into bite-sized chunks. In mixing bowl, combine corn, onion, zucchini, pepper, dressing and paprika. Mix well. Add fish bits and toss to coat with dressing.

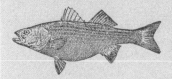

Striped Bass Facts

☞ *Striped bass are fast growing and long lived. In fact, a 125-pounder caught by commercial netters off the Atlantic coast was estimated to be 29 to 31 years old. So how old is a 10-pound striper? According to research done by fish biologists, a 10-pound striper, which would measure about 28 inches in length, would be 5 to 6 years old.*

STRIPER SALAD

Like most fish, striped bass taste best when they are under 10 pounds. Stripers of this weight range are moist and tender, and can be prepared in almost any manner: roasted whole, baked, barbecued, grilled or poached. This recipe, while delicious with leftover striped bass, is tasty with other types of leftover fish as well.

Serves: 6
Preparation Time: Under 15 minutes

- 3 cups cooked striped bass, in bite-sized pieces
- 1¹/₂ cups mayonnaise
- 1 cup diced celery
- 2 tablespoons Dijon mustard
- Salt and pepper
- 1 head lettuce
- 2 tomatoes, sliced
- 3 hard-boiled eggs, quartered

No Cooking Required: In mixing bowl, combine striped bass, mayonnaise, celery and mustard; mix thoroughly. Season with salt and pepper to taste. Line each plate or bowl with a bed of lettuce. Divide the fish mixture evenly between plates. Garnish each dish with tomatoes and hard-boiled eggs.

MIDDAY TROUT DELIGHT

I created this side dish on a backcountry fishing trip to Alaska. Two heart surgeons were in our fishing party. They commented that if they ate like this at home, they'd both be 20 pounds thinner! It's a healthy yet delectable dish.

Serves: 6
Cooking Time: Under 15 minutes

2 cups water
1 1/2 lbs. boneless, skinless trout fillets
2 heads lettuce
2 tomatoes, thinly sliced

1 onion, thinly sliced
Half of a cucumber, thinly sliced
1 cup balsamic vinaigrette dressing or other oil-and-vinegar dressing

For Stovetop or Surface Cooking: In large skillet, heat water to boiling over high heat. Add trout; reduce heat to low and simmer for 3 to 4 minutes on each side. Remove skillet from heat and keep the fish in the liquid while preparing salad; the fillets will continue to cook.

Line 6 individual plates with a layer of lettuce leaves. Divide sliced tomatoes, onion and cucumber between the plates, arranging them attractively. Drain fish fillets; divide into 6 equal portions and place on top of the vegetables. Drizzle a generous 2 tablespoons dressing on each plate and serve immediately.

Note: If I plan on being streamside for the day, I like to prep the vegetables before heading out. I cut and place the cucumber, onion, tomatoes and lettuce leaves all in one plastic bag.

PHARAOH LAKE POTATO SALAD

One of the best remote lakes we've ever fished is Pharaoh Lake in New York's Adirondack Mountains. The hike in is a long one; the narrow-winding trail weaves through the forest for many miles before emerging onto one of the most beautiful and peaceful lakes I have ever visited. The shoreline is covered with lean-tos for campers who want to spend the night. It was here while fishing the lake and its tributaries for native brook trout that we first tried this recipe.

Serves: 2
Cooking Time: 30 to 60 minutes

2 large white or red-skinned potatoes, cut into quarters
2 eggs
2 cups water
1/4 cup diced wild onion tops or scallion tops

1/4 cup oil-and-vinegar dressing or Italian-style dressing
1 tablespoon mustard
2 tablespoons crumbled, cooked bacon or imitation bacon-flavored bits
Salt, pepper and paprika

For Stovetop or Surface Cooking: In saucepan, combine potatoes, eggs and water. Heat to boiling over high heat. Boil for 7 to 10 minutes, then remove the eggs and set aside to cool. Continue cooking potatoes until tender, about 15 minutes longer. Drain, cool and cut potatoes into small chunks. Peel eggs and cut into small bits. Mix onion tops, salad dressing and mustard in saucepan. Add potatoes, eggs and bacon; stir gently to mix thoroughly. Season with salt, pepper and paprika to taste.

SKILLET POTATO PATTIES

"Delicious!" is the consensus on this recipe. I've never made it without receiving accolades from those who are eating it. Depending on what pots and pans you've got at camp, this can be prepared in a skillet, Dutch oven or saucepan.

<u>Yield:</u> 6 servings
<u>Cooking Time:</u> 30 to 60 minutes

1¹/₂ cups water
 ¹/₃ cup powdered milk
   1 tablespoon butter-flavored sprinkles
1¹/₂ cups instant mashed potato flakes
   4 scallions (or the tops of wild onions), chopped
 ¹/₈ teaspoon onion salt
   3 tablespoons shortening, approx.

<u>For Stovetop or Surface Cooking:</u> In saucepan, blend water with powdered milk and butter-flavored sprinkles. Heat to boiling over medium heat. Remove from heat and add potato flakes, scallions and salt. Stir until potato flakes are moist and thoroughly mixed. Melt about 1 tablespoon of the shortening in skillet (or, if the saucepan you've mixed the potatoes in is your only pot, transfer mixture to a bowl, then clean out the pot and use that). When shortening is hot, add a scant ¹/₄ cup of potato mixture to skillet. Fry until browned on one side, then flip and brown second side. Transfer to a dish and set aside in a warm place while you fry remaining patties, adding additional shortening as needed.

TOMATOES 'N' RICE

Here's a quick, tasty and filling camp meal. While regular rice has a much better taste and texture, instant rice is well suited for the trail as it takes less time and much less water (often a precious resource when camping).

<u>Serves:</u> 2
<u>Cooking Time:</u> Under 30 minutes

1 tablespoon vegetable oil	1 green bell pepper, cored and diced
1 clove garlic, minced	1 onion, diced
1 can (28 oz.) crushed tomatoes	1 cup uncooked instant rice
¹/₄ teaspoon sugar	Salt and pepper

<u>For Stovetop or Surface Cooking:</u> In large skillet, heat oil over medium heat. Add garlic and stir to cook slightly; don't let it turn brown. Add crushed tomatoes with their juices, and the sugar; cook for about 10 minutes, stirring frequently. Add pepper, onion and rice and cook for 15 minutes longer, stirring occasionally. Season with salt and pepper to taste before serving.

Shore-lunch Tip

☞ *Instead of keeping one big fish for shore lunch, you're better off keeping several smaller fish. Not only do the smaller fish taste better, but you won't waste any fish. Working as a team, your group should fillet fish and prepare them for the frying pan as they're needed. As people start to get full, you simply plan accordingly and quit cleaning fish when you have the right amount of fillets.*

ROASTED WILD ONIONS and MUSHROOMS

This is a terrific recipe when time is limited, as you can assemble it and set it to roast while you take care of other camp matters. It makes a great side dish for almost any meal.

Wild Onions, Garlic & Ramps

☞ *Wild onions, garlic and ramps (wild leeks) all come from the Allium family and are found throughout the United States. They thrive in both sun and shade, and are found in both the forests and fields. The tiny flowers that appear at the tops of the plants can be white, red, yellow, pink or purple. All members of the wild onion family have a flat or hollow edible green stem and emit a distinct onion-like smell when cut. Both bulbs and stems are edible. Make sure you smell the distinct oniony or garlicky aroma; there are poisonous members of the lily family that look similar to wild onions and garlic but don't have that distinctive odor.*

continued on page 47

Serves: 4
Cooking Time: Under 30 minutes

- 1 lb. wild or domestic onions, chopped
- 1 lb. wild mushrooms such as chanterelles or morels, or store-bought mushrooms, sliced
- 1/4 cup butter (half of a stick)
- 1 teaspoon garlic powder
- 1/4 teaspoon salt
- 1/8 teaspoon pepper
- A splash of camp white wine
- For cooking over coals you will also need: Aluminum foil, grill grate

For Cooking Over Coals: Prepare campfire or grill. Lay out 4 squares of foil (12-inch squares). Divide onions evenly between the squares, piling them in the center. Top each pile of onions with one-quarter of the mushrooms. Place 1 tablespoon butter on each pile; sprinkle with garlic powder, salt, pepper, and a few drops of wine. Seal foil by bringing together 2 opposite

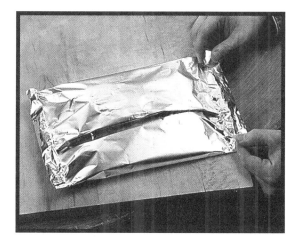

sides; fold down the top half-inch or so, and crease. Continue folding and creasing until you reach the top of the onion-mushroom mixture. Seal side seams in the same manner (see photo). Repeat with remaining packets. Place on grate over hot coals for about 20 minutes, turning once or twice.

For Dutch Oven Cooking: This can also be prepared in a Dutch oven. Preheat Dutch oven lid. Place all ingredients together in Dutch oven and stir to combine. Position Dutch oven over small bed of coals; place more hot coals on top of lid. Bake for 10 minutes. Remove lid and stir quickly; replace lid and bake for 10 minutes longer.

For Camp or Home Cooking in an Oven: Heat oven to 400°F. Combine all ingredients in roasting pan and stir to combine. Cover and bake for 20 minutes, stirring from time to time.

GRILLED CAMP VEGGIES

Here's a quick and tasty way to serve up delicious summer vegetables. Just skewer and grill . . . and there are no dishes to clean up! It's perfect for a summer's evening.

<u>Serves:</u> 4
<u>Cooking Time:</u> Under 30 minutes

Spice mixture:

  1 teaspoon ground cumin
1/2 teaspoon onion powder
1/2 teaspoon seasoned salt
1/4 teaspoon black pepper
1/8 teaspoon paprika

  2 medium zucchini, cut into 1-inch chunks
  2 medium summer squash, cut into 1-inch chunks
  2 tablespoons butter
1/2 teaspoon crumbled dried oregano
1/2 teaspoon snipped wild or domestic chives
    You will also need: Skewers; grill grate if cooking over coals

Optional Advance Preparation: Combine spice-mixture ingredients in large plastic food-storage bag; shake well to mix.

For Cooking Over Coals: Prepare grill. Add zucchini and summer squash chunks to bag with spices and toss to coat. Remove from bag and place onto skewers, alternating zucchini and summer squash chunks. Let sit for about 5 minutes. Melt butter in small skillet; add oregano and chives. Remove from heat. Drizzle butter mixture over skewered vegetables. Place skewers on grate about 6 inches from coals (or over medium heat if using gas grill). Cook for about 10 minutes, or until vegetables are just tender, turning occasionally.

For Camp or Home Cooking with a Broiler: Prepare and skewer vegetables as described above. Place under broiler and cook for about 10 minutes, turning several times.

continued from page 46

• *Ramps are wild leeks that grow to about 12 inches in height. They have broad, flat-leaved tops and taste like a strong leek. They don't form underground bulbs. Instead, their underground stems look like thin scallions. When you harvest them, peel off the outer skin. Remember that a little goes a long way.*

• *Wild garlic has thin stalks that can grow up to 2 feet tall. They can be harvested when the tops are brown and dry. Gently lift the tops and, for optimum flavor, sun-dry the segmented bulbs for a few days before using.*

• *Wild onions come in many varieties, and their green tops can be used in the same way as domestic scallions. Their stalks or leaves are thin and are hollow when cut. Like wild garlic, they can be harvested when the tops begin to dry in late summer.*

Making the Most of a Woodstove

☞ *Woodstove cookery isn't as easy as lighting a fire, letting it roar for awhile and then cooking on top! The fine art of cooking on a woodstove has much to do with the efficient management of the draft and damper adjustments. Here is a quick rundown of the major components of a woodstove.*

• The stovepipe damper's main purpose is to allow the smoke to leave the oven and exit through the flue. This can all be drastically affected by the outside temperature and weather, cleanliness of the chimney, and length of the flue.

• The oven damper is used to divert heat to warm the oven compartment;

continued on page 49

CORN ON THE COB

This is a traditional favorite in my family. This recipe will enhance any lunch or dinner you prepare with minimum effort and maximum results!

Serves: Per serving; make as many as needed
Cooking Time: Under 30 minutes

Fresh corn ears with husks intact
Butter or margarine, softened
Salt and pepper*
For cooking over coals you will also need: Aluminum foil, grill grate if available

For Cooking Over Coals: Prepare campfire or grill. Peel husks back from corn ears, but do not remove all the way. Pluck away the silk. Rub butter or margarine over corn kernels, and season to taste with salt and pepper. Smooth husks back over corn ears and wrap each ear with foil.

If grill grate is available, place wrapped corn on grate away from the flames; otherwise, place wrapped corn directly on a bed of coals. Cook for 10 to 15 minutes, turning occasionally.

For Camp or Home Cooking in an Oven: Heat oven to 400°F. Season and wrap ears of corn in foil as directed; this prevents butter from seeping out and burning in the oven. Place foil-wrapped ears on rimmed baking sheet. Bake for 10 to 12 minutes.

*Note: To spice up the corn, use a little less black pepper than you normally would and add a little cayenne pepper.

EASY CAMP TOMATO SAUCE

If you bring fresh tomatoes on your trip, here's a quick recipe for a delicious sauce to accompany any type of pasta. Since my time is of the essence when afield, I don't peel the tomatoes, opting for my grandmother's "Waste not, want not" adage. However, if you prefer, you can peel the tomatoes before cooking the sauce. Dunking them in a pot of simmering water first will make them much easier to peel.

Yield: 2 cups
Cooking Time: 30 to 60 minutes

1 tablespoon plus 1½ teaspoons olive oil
4 cloves garlic, minced

6 medium tomatoes, seeded and diced
¼ teaspoon salt
¼ teaspoon pepper

For Stovetop or Surface Cooking: In saucepan, heat oil over medium-low heat. Add garlic and sauté until just golden; don't let it turn brown. Stir in tomatoes and salt and let them come to a simmer. Adjust heat and simmer for about 30 minutes. Season with pepper and serve.

DOG 'N' BEAN CASSEROLE

This is a camp standard that I prepare often, whether we've pitched a tent or are just stopping for a quick camp lunch on the trail. It seems to please everyone.

Serves: 8 to 10
Cooking Time: Over 1 hour

3/4 lb. bacon, chopped	1 cup brown sugar
1 medium onion, chopped	1 cup ketchup
1 lb. hot dogs, sliced	1 tablespoon vinegar
1 can (15 1/2 oz.) kidney beans, drained	1 tablespoon mustard
1 can (11 oz.) pork and beans	1 teaspoon liquid smoke
1 can (15 1/2 oz.) navy beans, drained	You will also need: Dutch oven

For Dutch Oven Cooking: Prepare campfire; preheat Dutch oven lid in coals. In Dutch oven, brown bacon over medium heat, stirring occasionally. Drain off excess fat. Sauté onion in remaining fat until translucent. Add remaining ingredients and stir to combine. Place preheated lid on Dutch oven. Position Dutch oven over small bed of coals; place additional hot coals on top of lid. Bake for 45 to 60 minutes.

For Camp or Home Cooking in an Oven: Heat oven to 325°F. Fry bacon and onion as directed above. Combine all ingredients in casserole dish. Cover and bake for 55 minutes.

CAMP MACARONI and CHEESE

There are many prepackaged mac 'n' cheese mixes available in grocery stores. These can be very handy for a quick snack, accompaniment, or, in a larger portion, a full meal. But if you run out or have a hankering for the real thing, try this simple and delicious recipe.

Serves: 4 as a side dish, 2 as a main dish
Cooking Time: Under 15 minutes

8 oz. uncooked macaroni	2 tablespoon butter
About 2 quarts water	1 tablespoon grated onion
1 cup shredded cheddar cheese	1/8 teaspoon paprika
1/4 cup grated Parmesan cheese	1 cup milk

For Stovetop or Surface Cooking: In saucepan, cook macaroni in boiling water until tender but not mushy; drain well. Return macaroni to saucepan and place over low heat. Add remaining ingredients in the order listed. (If you can't drain the macaroni completely, watch the amount of milk you add so as not to make too thin.) Continue stirring until cheese has melted. Serve warm.

continued from page 48

in order for damping to work properly, the fire needs to be fairly hot.

• The draft is an opening on the bottom of the firebox that controls the amount of air feeding the fire. The more open it is, the hotter the fire will burn.

• The check draft is an opening near the top of the firebox that allows fresh air into the top of the firebox; this air controls the flames and keeps them "in check."

Oftentimes the woodstove is also used as a source of heat within the cabin. To increase the heat radiating from the woodstove, close the oven damper. This way, more of the heat will go up instead of keeping the lower oven warm. In addition, if you take a large piece (or several large pieces) of aluminum foil, make a sturdy frame around it and place it behind the stove, more heat will be reflected to the front.

MAIN DISH
CAMP RECIPES

My first experience with hunting upland birds over dogs was in 1987 when our chocolate Lab, Stoney, had finished her training and was ready for her first real hunt. To celebrate the experience, we packed the Suburban full of hunting gear and headed to the eastern plains of Montana.

During our 5-day hunt, our 1½-year-old pup was turned into a seasoned gun dog. Even though she had never seen a chukar, it only took a few flocks to flush in front of her before that scent passed from her highly sensitive nose directly to her brain, where it was etched forever. It was also her first encounter with sage grouse. It's a memory we'll never forget:

While hunting an abandoned grass field on a grain farm, Stoney ran past an old wagon wheel and screeched to a halt. She headed back to the broken wooden wheel that lay against a large rock. She half-pointed at the wheel with her head cocked and looked from us to the wheel and back again. We were sure she had cornered a badger, skunk or some other mammal and was confused by its refusal to leave. But as we got closer, we spotted a large sage grouse cowering between the wheel and the rock. Each time Stoney stuck her nose through the spokes to get a better sniff of the stubborn bird, it would try to take a piece of her nose off.

Perplexed that the bird would not flush, Stoney finally stuck her head deep through the spokes of the wheel. Rather than flying off, the bird lunged at Stoney, latched onto her lip and hung on for dear life as the poor dog shook her head back and forth. The instant she shook it free, the bird was airborne, and I quickly shot it. As the bird fell to the ground, Stoney ran to retrieve it. But rather than picking it up, she slowly began to kick the bird toward us! Then, with all the bravery she could muster, she carefully picked up the bird, trotted over to us, and dropped it. Although the incident didn't affect her enthusiasm for flushing sage grouse, her retrieval of these birds was always more cautious than with any other game bird.

If you've ever hunted the eastern portion of Montana you'll know that there aren't many crop fields, grasslands, river bottoms or sagebrush flats that don't harbor game birds. The action was nonstop the entire trip, and each day we filled our bag limits with a variety of birds. Many were given to the landowners to thank them for allowing us to hunt their property. What I wasn't prepared for, however, was the kindness and hospitality extended to us. Delighted to get the birds, these ranchers and farmers often invited us to join them for dinner. It wasn't long before we were exchanging recipes.

In this section you'll find ways to prepare all types of birds, fish and game as main meals. Whether you're at deer camp and want to celebrate a hunter's harvest with Venison Filet with Morels, or you want to prepare a young angler's catch of ol' whisker-face with Catfish Noodle Bake, I know you'll find a recipe to your liking. If you are at a summer camp along the seashore, don't miss my recipe for Grill-Roasted Striped Bass or melt-in-your-mouth Grilled Lobster. I know you'll enjoy these recipes — they're quick and easy!

Game-Bird Recipes

BARBECUED MALLARD DUCK BREASTS À L'ORANGE

No matter what camp, cabin or lodge I have prepared this recipe in, my guests or companions have always raved about its taste. Try this one the next time you're on a getaway to your cabin.

<u>Serves:</u> 2
<u>Cooking Time:</u> 30 to 60 minutes

4 skin-on duck breasts (6 to 8 oz. each)
2 oranges
3 tablespoons honey
1 tablespoon lemon juice
   You will also need: Grill grate, basting brush

<u>For Cooking Over Coals:</u> Prepare grill or campfire. With sharp knife, slash skin of the breasts 3 or 4 times in parallel lines. Make sure you do not cut too deeply; you want to cut only the skin and not the flesh. Then do the same in the opposite (perpendicular) way to score the skin of the duck, in crisscross fashion. In this way, the fat from underneath the skin will be able to melt so the outer skin can become crisp.

To get maximum juice from the oranges, roll them on a hard surface while exerting some pressure. Squeeze oranges into shallow, nonmetallic dish; transfer 2 table-spoons of the juice to a small bowl and set aside. Add duck breasts, skin side up, to the dish with the rest of the juice. Marinate for about 20 minutes. Add honey and lemon juice to bowl with the 2 tablespoons of orange juice; this will be used as a basting glaze.

Heat grill grate over coals. Place breasts on grate, skin side down. Baste with glaze. Grill for about 5 minutes, brushing occasionally with glaze. Turn and grill second side for 6 to 8 minutes, basting frequently. When breasts are desired doneness, remove from grill and let sit for 5 minutes so the juices distribute evenly. Serve immediately.

Ducks & Weather

☞ *In sunny weather, ducks tend to fly early and late in the day and sit tight during the mid-day. But when skies are overcast, the morning and evening activity period lasts longer; when the ceiling is very low, they may fly all day long.*

☞ *Puddle ducks, like mallards, are usually found in calm water. In windy weather, they seek shelter along a lee shore.*

SOY-GRILLED RUFFED GROUSE

Ruffed grouse is a challenging game bird, and to come back to the cabin with 3 or 4 is quite a morning's feat. For the days afield when you and your companions have hit into the birds well, here's a savory way to prepare these delectable deep-woods birds.

Serves: 3 or 4

Cooking Time: Under 15 minutes

Basting sauce:

2/3 cup soy sauce

  2 teaspoons wine

  1 teaspoon ground ginger

  2 cloves garlic, minced

  3 or 4 dressed ruffed grouse (about 2 lbs. each), skin on
     You will also need: Grill grate, basting brush

Optional Advance Preparation: Combine basting-sauce ingredients in jar or other sealable container. Keep cool until used.

For Cooking Over Coals: Prepare grill or campfire; heat grill grate over coals. Cut grouse into halves. Place grouse on grate, skin side down. Baste with sauce. Grill for about 5 minutes on each side, brushing continuously with sauce.

GRILLED QUAIL

This recipe was prepared for a bunch of hungry tailgaters in a parking lot prior to a football game. Its ease in preparation allows you to grill quail over a fire from a lean-to, a cabin, lodge or even something as exotic as on the back of a pickup truck for a Jets game!

Serves: 3 or 4

Cooking Time: Under 15 minutes

6 to 8 dressed quail (4 to 8 oz. each), skinless

2 cups Italian dressing

Garlic powder, onion powder, salt and pepper

You will also need: Grill grate

For Cooking Over Coals: Prepare campfire or grill. Split quail down the backbone and open out; for additional grilled flavor, press the breasts of the birds to flatten the split carcass. Place quail in large zipper-style plastic bag or in nonmetallic bowl and add just enough dressing to coat. Save remaining dressing for basting while grilling. You can let the birds sit in the dressing while the grill or fire is being prepared.

When coals are ready, remove quail from dressing and season with garlic powder, onion powder, salt and pepper to taste. Place quail on grate over hot coals and cook for 5 to 7 minutes on each side, basting frequently with reserved Italian dressing.

Ruffed Grouse vs. Sage Grouse

☞ *Ruffed grouse are considered among the tastiest of wild birds. They average about 2 pounds. Their bigger cousins, the sage grouse, weigh 3 to 6 pounds. If you're using sage grouse in a recipe written for ruffed grouse, plan on increasing the other ingredients proportionately to accommodate the larger bird.*

TURKEY ROLLS SUPREME

Whether you prepare this recipe in camp, at the cabin or at home, I recommend that you make enough for seconds. I will say no more. You've been warned.

<u>Serves:</u> 4 or 5
<u>Cooking Time:</u> 30 to 60 minutes

1¹/₂ cups diced cooked turkey
 ¹/₂ cup shredded cheddar cheese
　2 tablespoons chopped onion
　1 tablespoon milk
　1 teaspoon paprika
　　Half to 1 can (10³/₄ oz.) condensed cream of mushroom soup
　1 tube (8 oz.) refrigerated crescent rolls
　　You will also need: Dutch oven, aluminum foil

<u>For Dutch Oven Cooking:</u> Prepare campfire; preheat Dutch oven lid in coals. Line inside of Dutch oven with foil; set aside. In mixing bowl, combine turkey, cheese, onion, milk, paprika and half of the mushroom soup. Mix well and add additional soup as necessary; the mixture should be neither too dry nor too runny.

Cover a large, flat work surface with foil or plastic wrap. Unroll crescent roll dough. Flatten it out to form a 15 x 13-inch rectangle. Spread turkey mixture down center of dough, leaving about 1 inch clear on edges. Roll up dough and seal edge with a little water. Slice the roll in half and place the halves, side by side but not touching, in lined Dutch oven. Place preheated lid on Dutch oven. Position Dutch oven over small bed of coals; place additional hot coals on top of lid. Bake for about 25 minutes, or until tops of rolls are golden brown. Remove rolls from Dutch oven and let stand for about 5 minutes before slicing into serving-sized pieces.

<u>For Camp or Home Cooking in an Oven:</u> Heat oven to 375°F. Prepare roll as directed above, but do not cut in half. Place on baking sheet. Bake for 20 minutes, or until golden brown. Remove from oven and let stand for about 5 minutes before slicing into serving-sized pieces.

About Freeze-Dried Foods

☞ *Although they are expensive, freeze-dried foods are lightweight and easy to cook. Some dishes you can whip up in a jiffy include chili, beef stew, peas, potatoes, pudding, applesauce and many soups. When you're cooking freeze-dried meals, be sure to follow directions exactly as they are printed.*

GRILLED GROUSE

One of Peter's buddies is a big-time grouse hunter and we often hunted grouse on day trips throughout New York State. I always brought a portable grill on these ventures. I knew that when we were fortunate enough to get a few birds, we would take a break in the middle of the day. While I prepared the grouse, the guys would break out the cheese, crackers and other amenities we brought along. You can even prepare this over an open pit fire or anywhere else you can place a grill over a flame.

Serves: 4 or 5
Cooking Time: Under 30 minutes

4   dressed ruffed grouse (about 2 lbs. each), skin on
1/2 cup butter (1 stick), melted
    Salt and pepper
8   slices bacon
    You will also need: Grill grate, basting brush, aluminum foil

For Cooking Over Coals: Prepare campfire or grill. Cut grouse into halves. Brush grouse with some of the melted butter, and season with salt and pepper to taste. Place on grate over hot coals, skin side up. Grill for 7 to 10 minutes on each side, basting frequently with additional melted butter. When almost done, turn the birds skin side up and place bacon slices on top of each half. Place foil on top of the grouse to form a tent. Cook until bacon is done. Serve immediately.

For Camp or Home Cooking with a Broiler: Arrange grouse skin side up on broiler pan. Brush grouse with some of the melted butter, and season with salt and pepper to taste. Place about 3 inches from broiler element and cook, turning once and basting frequently with additional melted butter, until almost done. When almost done, turn the birds skin side up and place bacon slices on top of each half. Move broiler pan down one level; if your broiler has a "low" setting, turn broiler to low. Cook until bacon is done; watch for any bacon grease that might hit the broiling unit. If this happens, immediately move the rack down one level again. As soon as bacon is crisp, serve immediately.

Grouse Tails

☞ *You can determine whether a ruffed grouse you've harvested is a male or female by examining the tail feathers. Begin by spreading the tail feathers into a fan. Now look at the outside edge of the fan. Males have a solid band of black around the entire margin. In females, the two center feathers do not have a distinct black band.*

☞ *Ruffed grouse have two distinct color phases, both of which may occur in the same family. The red-phase birds have a mottled, brownish body and chestnut-colored tail. Gray-phase birds have a mottled, grayish body and gray tail.*

BAKED PHEASANT CASSEROLE

While pheasant hunting in Iowa a few years back, I had the chance to try this recipe. Cumin adds a nice zing to this flavorful dish; try it if you like spicy meals.

<u>Serves:</u> 4
<u>Cooking Time:</u> 1^{1}/$_{2}$ to 2 hours

- 2 lbs. pheasant meat, cut into 1- to 2-inch chunks
- 1 cup cracker crumbs
- ^{1}/$_{2}$ cup butter (1 stick), divided
- 1 can (10^{3}/$_{4}$ oz.) condensed cream of mushroom soup
- 1 cup mayonnaise
- 5 teaspoons cumin
  Salt and pepper
  You will also need: Dutch oven

<u>For Dutch Oven Cooking:</u> Prepare campfire; preheat Dutch oven lid in coals. Dredge pheasant chunks in cracker crumbs. In Dutch oven, melt 2 tablespoons of the butter over medium heat. When butter is sizzling, add a batch of pheasant chunks and fry until golden brown on all sides. Transfer browned pheasant to dish; repeat with remaining pheasant, adding butter as needed. When all pheasant has been browned, return all pieces to Dutch oven. In mixing bowl, combine soup, mayonnaise, cumin, and salt and pepper to taste. Stir well and pour over pheasant pieces. Place preheated lid on Dutch oven. Position Dutch oven over small bed of coals; place additional hot coals on top of lid. Bake for about 1^{1}/$_{2}$ hours, replenishing coals as necessary.

<u>For Camp or Home Cooking in an Oven:</u> Heat oven to 350°F. Dredge pheasant chunks in cracker crumbs. In skillet, melt 2 tablespoons of the butter over medium heat. When butter is sizzling, add a batch of pheasant chunks and fry until golden brown on all sides. Transfer browned pheasant to casserole dish; repeat with remaining pheasant, adding butter as needed. In mixing bowl, combine soup, mayonnaise, cumin, and salt and pepper to taste. Stir well and pour over pheasant pieces. Cover and bake for 1^{1}/$_{2}$ hours.

19th Century Pheasants

☞ *After numerous unsuccessful stocking attempts, no one imagined that the 26 ring-necked pheasants stocked in Oregon in 1882 would result in a harvest of nearly 50,000 of the magnificent birds only a decade later. The remarkable adaptability of this Chinese import was demonstrated time after time as the birds were introduced across the country. They're now found in about 40 states and 7 Canadian provinces.*

INDIAN PHEASANT STIR-FRY

One of the best culinary techniques we have inherited from the Far East is stir-frying. This cooking method enhances the flavors of food as the ingredients are seared quickly at a very high heat. Like most stir-fry recipes this pheasant meal is cooked in one pan, making preparation easy on the trail or at camp. The recipe below can also be prepared with other game birds such as turkey, grouse, chukar or partridge; you could also use chicken or rabbit.

Serves: 2 or 3
Cooking Time: Under 15 minutes

Marinade:

1/4 cup soy sauce
2 tablespoons lime juice
1 tablespoon honey
1/4 teaspoon curry powder

2 pheasant breasts (about 1 lb.), cut into 3/4-inch cubes
1 green bell pepper, cored and chopped
1 carrot, chopped
1/2 cup bean sprouts
1 tablespoon vegetable oil
Hot cooked rice or noodles

Optional Advance Preparation: In small jar, combine marinade ingredients. Keep cool until used.

For Stovetop or Surface Cooking: In mixing bowl or zipper-style plastic bag, combine pheasant, green pepper, carrot, bean sprouts and marinade. Toss thoroughly so all ingredients are well coated. Heat skillet or Dutch oven over high heat. Drain and discard excess marinade from pheasant and vegetables. Add oil to skillet. When oil is hot, add pheasant and vegetables. Stir fry for 6 to 8 minutes, or until vegetables are tender. Serve with rice or noodles.

SAUTÉED APPLE GROUSE

For both sport and eating pleasure, the fast-flying, hard-to-hit grouse is second to none. This recipe is easy to prepare and very tasty, and will bring many "That's delicious!" accolades from fellow campers.

Serves: 2
Cooking Time: 30 to 60 minutes

2 dressed grouse (about 1 lb. each), skin on
1 teaspoon garlic powder
Salt and pepper
2 tablespoons vegetable oil
1 small onion, chopped

1 stalk celery, chopped
1/2 cup dry white wine
1/4 to 1/2 cup water
1/4 cup raisins
1 medium apple, peeled, cored and chopped

For Stovetop or Surface Cooking: Cut grouse into halves. Sprinkle with garlic powder, and salt and pepper to taste; rub seasonings in with your fingers. Heat skillet or Dutch oven over medium-high heat and add the oil. Add grouse; fry until browned on all sides. Add onion and celery; cook until tender, stirring vegetables occasionally. Add wine and water; let the size of the pan dictate how much water to add in (or let your palate decide!). There needs to be enough liquid to let the grouse braise. Cover and reduce heat; simmer for about 30 minutes. Mix in the raisins and apple and simmer for 10 minutes longer.

FRIED QUAIL

Texas has long been synonymous with whitetail deer hunting. But what most people don't realize is that second to deer, Texas' most popular game quarry is the bobwhite quail. I've hunted bobwhites all through the South, as well as mountain quail in California, and Gamble's quail in New Mexico and Arizona. But none of these offers the quality and quantity found in the Lone Star State. If you ever get the opportunity, plan to hunt quail in Texas and don't forget to take this recipe with you.

Serves: 2
Cooking Time: Under 15 minutes

  4 dressed quail (4 to 8 oz. each), skin on
  1 cup flour
    Salt and pepper
1/2 to 1 cup butter (1 to 2 sticks)

For Stovetop or Surface Cooking: Cut quail into halves. Place flour in large plastic food-storage bag; add salt and pepper to taste and shake well to mix. Add quail halves, shaking to coat. In Dutch oven, melt 1 stick of the butter over medium-high heat; if it is not at least 1/2 inch deep in the Dutch oven, add more. Fry quail until golden brown, 4 to 5 minutes, turning once.

SOUTHERN FRIED QUAIL

During a deer and quail hunt at Burnt Pine Plantation in Georgia, our host fried up some quail at the lodge one evening. Since then, fried quail has been one of my favorite game bird recipes. This one is among my top-five favorite quail recipes.

Serves: 3
Cooking Time: Under 30 minutes

  6 dressed quail (4 to 8 oz. each), skinless
  2 eggs
11/4 cups milk
 1/2 cup all-purpose flour
 1/2 cup cornmeal
  1 teaspoon salt
    Vegetable oil

For Stovetop or Surface Cooking: Split quail into halves; set aside. In mixing bowl or flat dish, beat together eggs, milk, flour, cornmeal and salt. Add enough oil to a large pot or Dutch oven to completely cover the quail. Heat oil over medium-high heat. Test the oil by dropping a bit of batter into the skillet; when the oil is hot enough the batter will bubble and begin to cook instantly. Dip quail into batter, letting excess drip off. Cook quail until golden brown on all sides, 8 to 10 minutes. Drain on paper towel–lined plate.

Quail Dogs

☞ *Most experienced quail hunters regard pointing dogs as an indispensable tool. The classic quail dog is a big runner, such as an English pointer or a southern-bred English setter. But closer-working dogs, like Gordon setters and Brittanys, may work better in heavy cover.*

☞ *Hunters who pursue a wide variety of upland birds, as well as waterfowl, often try to buy the perfect "all-purpose" dog. Unfortunately, no such dog exists. You'll do better by selecting a dog well suited to your primary type of hunting, rather than one that will do a fair to poor job on several types.*

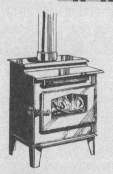

Fueling a Woodstove

☞ For fuel, you'll need both kindling and firewood. The general rule to follow is to use softwoods for kindling, and hardwood fuel for a long-burning fire. Some of the more common softwoods include balsam, fir, poplar, spruce and pine. These softwoods are easy to light because they are resinous and they burn quickly. Some of the more common hardwoods include oak, hickory, ash, beech, maple, black locust and dogwood. All of these woods will provide a strong, slow-burning flame. Be careful if you use a lot of softwoods, as they can cause a dangerous buildup of creosote in the chimney flue.

PAN TURKEY 'N' STUFFING

We were hunting turkeys in Texas when I first tried this recipe. I had been to a village outside camp a few days before and picked up a small box of stuffing mix and some fresh vegetables. The night I prepared this recipe, on our way back to camp, we had just seen at least 100 Rio Grande turkeys fly up from a field to roost in the trees. It was such a sight to see. The sun was setting and as more and more birds got settled in the upper branches, the skyline visible through the trees disappeared. With the decreasing light in the sky, the tops of the trees seemed to turn black. Needless to say, it was easy to decide where we were going to start out our hunt the next morning.

Serves: 2
Cooking Time: Under 30 minutes

- 3 tablespoon butter
- 1 medium onion, diced
- 1 small green or red bell pepper, cored and diced
- 1/2 to 3/4 lb. turkey breast, cubed
- 1 small tomato, seeded and diced
- 1 chicken bouillon cube
- 1/2 cup water
- 1/2 cup seasoned stuffing mix
- Salt and pepper

For Stovetop or Surface Cooking: In large skillet or Dutch oven, melt butter over medium heat. Add onion and bell pepper; sauté until tender. Add turkey cubes and cook for 5 to 7 minutes. Add tomato and cook for 1 or 2 minutes, stirring frequently. Add bouillon cube and water. Stir until cube dissolves; add a little more water if necessary. Add stuffing mix and stir until all liquid is absorbed. Season with salt and pepper if necessary.

FRIED GOOSE BREASTS

We lease a 100-acre piece of land called Shireforge Farm that is only minutes from where we live. It offers an excellent population of geese and waterfowl that use the lands and ponds on and around it. Every season, we take a half-dozen or so honkers there. During our late season in January, I intentionally shot a couple of young geese during our first snowstorm of the season. They were low and I lead them far enough to prevent any pellets from entering the breast — making them the perfect choice for this recipe. This size goose (the smallest birds in the flock, which usually fly in the back of the group) is always perfect for frying. It's hard to serve up goose — quickly — any better than this.

Giant Canada Geese

☞ *Biologists disagree on the number of subspecies, but some say there are more than a dozen. The largest are the giant Canada geese, which average 11 pounds. The smallest subspecies are the cackling geese, which weigh about 3 pounds.*

☞ *Large powerful wings enable geese to take flight very quickly, even though some giant Canada geese can reach weights of 15 pounds. Once in flight, geese are easily recognized by their slower wingbeat when compared to the fast wingbeat of ducks.*

<u>Serves:</u> 3 or 4
<u>Cooking Time:</u> Under 30 minutes

  2 boneless, skinless goose breast halves (about 1 lb. each)
1/4 cup cornmeal
1/4 cup all-purpose flour, plus 2 tablespoons for thickening
1/4 cup bacon drippings or vegetable oil
1/4 cup milk or water
     Salt and pepper

For Stovetop or Surface Cooking: Slice goose breasts across the grain into cutlets of about 1/4-inch thickness. Combine cornmeal and the 1/4 cup flour in large plastic food-storage bag. Add goose breast pieces, shaking to coat.

In large skillet, heat bacon drippings over medium-high heat. Test to make sure the drippings are sizzling hot by dropping a pinch of the flour mixture in the skillet. If the flour sizzles immediately, the drippings are hot enough. Add a single layer of goose pieces to skillet and cook for about 1 minute on each side. Transfer to heated dish; set aside while you fry remaining pieces. When all pieces have been cooked, discard all but 2 tablespoons drippings from skillet. Stir in the remaining 2 tablespoons flour to make a roux (paste). When the paste is smooth, add milk, a little at a time, stirring constantly. Cook for a minute or so to make a gravy. Season the gravy with salt and pepper to taste. Pour gravy over the goose cutlets and serve hot.

Small-Game Recipes

PETER RABBIT STEW 'N' DUMPLINGS

One of my husband Peter's favorite adages about how to hunt deer when heavy hunting pressure is on is, "If you want to find deer, hunt them like rabbits." During last year's deer season I decided to do just that. I left my treestand and started to walk through some of the heavy brush when I stopped at one large, thorny thicket. I was looking over the swampy field in front of me when out from the thorn bush darted a large cottontail. He took a few hops and stopped right in front of me. As soon as I saw him I thought to myself, "Hmmm — he'd make some good eating!" I was still contemplating this when from the corner of my eye I saw a 4-point buck explode from the same patch of cover. In three leaps, he was gone. As I looked back at the rabbit I realized that not paying attention to the job at hand cost me a buck.

Here's a recipe that we've enjoyed at camp for all the rabbits that didn't get away! This recipe is one that simmers for a while, so plan on it when dinnertime is not rushed.

<u>Serves:</u> 8 to 10
<u>Cooking Time:</u> 1¹/₂ to 2 hours

1¹/₂ cups all-purpose flour	**Dumplings:**
1 teaspoon pepper	2 cups all-purpose flour
1 teaspoon Adobo seasoning	1 tablespoon baking powder
2 cottontail rabbits, cut for stewing (about 5 lbs. total)	¹/₂ teaspoon salt
³/₄ cup vegetable oil	1 tablespoon minced wild onion tops or scallion tops
2 quarts water	1 cup milk (can use reconstituted dry milk)
6 yellow onions, cut into halves	1 tablespoon butter, melted
6 carrots, cut into 2-inch sections	1 egg
1 tablespoon salt	
1 can corn (15¹/₄ oz.), drained	

<u>*Optional Advance Preparation:*</u> If you like, you can prepare 2 separate bags with the dry ingredients: one bag with the 1¹/₂ cups flour, the pepper and Adobo seasoning (for coating the rabbit) and another with the 2 cups flour, the baking powder and salt for the dumplings.

<u>*For Stovetop or Surface Cooking:*</u> In large plastic food-storage bag, combine the 1¹/₂ cups flour, the pepper and Adobo seasoning, shaking well to mix. Coat rabbit pieces with seasoned flour, shaking off any excess. In Dutch oven, heat oil over

medium-high heat until sizzling hot. Add a layer of rabbit and brown on all sides. Transfer browned rabbit to paper towel–lined plate and set aside while you brown remaining rabbit. When all pieces have been browned, drain oil from Dutch oven.

Add water to Dutch oven and heat to simmering. (Note: This process will move a little faster if you have a second pot or pan that you can use to heat the water while you are frying the rabbit in the first stage; carefully pour hot water into Dutch oven when ready.) When water is hot, add fried rabbit, onions, carrots and salt. The water should just cover all the ingredients; adjust if necessary. Cover Dutch oven and let stew simmer for about 1 1/2 hours, or until carrots are cooked. At the end of cooking time, add corn and let simmer while you prepare the dumplings.

To prepare the dumplings, combine the 2 cups flour, the baking powder and salt in a mixing bowl. Stir in the wild onion tops. In small bowl, mix together milk, melted butter and egg, making sure the butter isn't too hot. Pour liquid ingredients into the dry ingredients and quickly combine; the batter should be stiff.

Dip a large spoon into the simmering gravy of the stew, then scoop out dumpling-size portions of the batter and drop into the liquid. Do this until the dumplings cover the entire surface of the stew, but don't overcrowd or the dumplings won't cook properly. Cover Dutch oven and let cook for about 10 minutes. Serve immediately.

HEDGEROW RABBIT SAUTÉ

Whenever we shoot sporting clays, my husband Peter quickly dispatches every rabbit target presented. One time I asked why he was so good at this. He replied, "You're kidding. I'm Italian. It was standard for my grandfather to slap anyone in the back of the head and mutter a dozen profanities about your shooting ability if you missed a rabbit on a family hunt. He would end each slap with a saying in broken English, 'Bada-bing, bada-boom-like-a-that. He's-a-dead!'" So, with rabbit hunting skills drilled in at an early age, Peter continues to fill our pantry with this sweet-tasting and flavorful small-game staple.

Serves: 3
Cooking Time: 30 to 60 minutes

1/4 cup all-purpose flour	1 medium onion, sliced
Garlic powder	1 medium green bell pepper, cored and sliced
Salt and pepper	1 can (6 oz.) tomato paste
1 boned cottontail rabbit (about 2 1/2 lbs.), cut into 1-inch chunks	1 cup water
2 tablespoons vegetable oil	1 or 2 tablespoons red wine, optional
	1/4 teaspoon crumbled dried marjoram

For Stovetop or Surface Cooking: Place flour in large plastic food-storage bag; add garlic powder, salt and pepper to taste and shake well to mix. Coat rabbit chunks with seasoned flour. Heat oil in large skillet or Dutch oven over medium-high heat. Add rabbit chunks and brown on all sides. Transfer browned rabbit chunks to dish; set aside. Add onion and green pepper to skillet; sauté for 3 to 5 minutes, stirring well to loosen any browned bits from the bottom of the skillet. In jar or other container, combine tomato paste, water and wine; mix well. Add tomato paste mixture, marjoram and browned rabbit chunks to skillet. Reduce heat and cover. Simmer for 30 to 45 minutes.

Venison Recipes

Morel Mushrooms

☞ Morel mushrooms are a wonderful delicacy that must be cleaned properly before eating. The simplest way is to slice them lengthwise, and dunk in heavily salted, heated water. There are all sorts of critters and dirt that can find a nice home in these delectable fungi. Jostle them around in the pot for about 5 minutes, then drain on a paper towel. Morels are best eaten fresh, but can be dried for later use, too.

VENISON FILET with MORELS

Every time I take any big-game animal (especially a whitetail), I remove the tenderloin as quickly as possible. Even though I have been doing this for years, I find that each time I am removing the tenderloins I am always planning in my head how I will cook this choicest of all the cuts. One way to enhance tenderloin to its max is with this recipe!

Serves: 3 or 4
Cooking Time: Under 30 minutes

  1 cup butter (2 sticks), divided
  2 tablespoons pepper
  1 lb. venison tenderloin, cut into 1/2-inch-thick medallions
1/2 cup plus 2 teaspoons all-purpose flour, divided
  8 oz. fresh morel mushrooms, chopped
1/3 cup sherry
  2 tablespoons freshly chopped chives or wild onion tops
1/3 cup beef broth
     Salt and pepper

For Stovetop or Surface Cooking: In Dutch oven, heat 1 stick of the butter over medium-high heat until sizzling. Press the pepper into the loin steaks and then dip them into the 1/2 cup flour. Add to hot butter and sauté until just browned on both sides. Take care not to overcook the venison; it should be about medium-rare. Remove venison from Dutch oven and keep warm.

Add remaining butter, mushrooms, sherry and chives to Dutch oven. Cook for 5 to 7 minutes, or until morels are tender. Meanwhile, combine remaining 2 teaspoons flour and beef broth in small bowl, stirring to blend and remove any lumps. When mushrooms are tender, add broth mixture, stirring constantly. Cook, stirring constantly, until sauce thickens. Season sauce with salt and pepper to taste. Divide venison steaks between plates and top with mushroom sauce.

EASY VENISON GOULASH

You may substitute a less-tender cut of venison for the loin steak in this recipe; simply simmer it for about an hour before adding the beans.

Serves: 2
Cooking Time: 30 to 60 minutes

1 tablespoon vegetable oil	3/4 cup water
8 oz. venison loin steak, cut into 1/2-inch cubes	1 can (8 oz.) red kidney beans, drained
1/2 cup all-purpose flour, plus a little additional to thicken sauce	Salt and pepper
	Hot cooked rice or noodles for serving, optional
2 medium onions, chopped	
1 single-serve package dry tomato soup mix	

For Stovetop or Surface Cooking: In large skillet or Dutch oven, heat oil over medium-high heat. Coat venison cubes with flour, shaking to remove excess. Add venison to skillet and brown on all sides. Add onions, soup mix and water. Reduce heat and simmer for about 30 minutes. Add beans; cook for 10 minutes longer. Season to taste with salt and pepper. If the mixture is too watery, add a little flour to thicken. Serve over hot cooked rice or noodles.

RIVER BOTTOM VENISON TERIYAKI

We were hunting mule deer in Wyoming when I prepared this recipe from a nice 10-point whitetail buck that Peter shot. Peter knew a great spot along the cottonwoods that lined the riverbanks. As the buck emerged from the thick cover of a gully some 100 or so yards away, Peter used a soft grunt to get the buck's attention and bring him within bow range. While the buck sported a 125-class 5x5 rack, it turned out it was only 2 1/2 years old. As you can imagine, this deer turned out to be quite good eating!

Serves: 2
Cooking Time: 30 to 60 minutes

8 oz. venison loin, cut into 1-inch cubes	1/4 cup teriyaki sauce
Half of a medium onion, chopped	1/4 teaspoon ground ginger
1 clove garlic, minced	1 cup cooked rice

For Stovetop or Surface Cooking: In zipper-style plastic bag, combine venison, onion, garlic, teriyaki sauce and ginger. Mix thoroughly and let marinate for about 10 minutes. Heat skillet over medium-high heat. With slotted spoon or your fingers, remove venison from the bag and add it to the hot skillet. Cook, turning often, until nicely seared. Add remaining mixture from bag. Cook, stirring frequently, for 2 to 3 minutes, until onions are tender-crisp. Push meat and onions to one side of the skillet and place cooked rice in the other half. Let it heat through, stirring frequently. Serve immediately.

Pre-Cooked Noodles or Rice

Depending upon how long you're at camp or on the trail, rice and noodles can be prepared ahead of time and sealed in an airtight package. This saves not only time during meal preparation, but also saves ever-precious fresh water. Precooked noodles or rice need only be reheated in a hot skillet with a little bit of fresh water or oil. If you have a vacuum-sealer, it will make storing the items for the trip much easier. Be sure to keep precooked rice or noodles in the cooler (or refrigerator) until you use them.

EASY VENISON ROAST

Each year at deer camp, one of our group of hunters donates the deer they take as "camp meat" (we rotate this from year to year, taking turns). The camp deer feeds all the hunters during our stay; any leftover meat goes to the person who shot it. On such occasions, it is nice to prepare a roast for the camp. Here is a simple one that can be prepared either in a regular oven, or in a Dutch oven over the fire.

Do Some Good

☞ *In many states hunters are allowed to take more than one deer per year. Most often, these "bonus tags" are for antlerless deer. But what should you do if your family can't possibly eat all the deer you can legally harvest? Simple — contact the folks at the nonprofit organization, Farmers And Hunters Feeding The Hungry. They'll tell you if your state has a program for donating deer to the needy. Check out their website: www.fhfh.org for more information.*

Serves: 8 to 10
Cooking Time: Over 1 hour

- 1 4- to 5-lb. venison roast
  Salt and pepper
- 2 lemons (one halved, one sliced)
- 12 slices bacon
- 2 onions, chopped
- 2 tablespoons Worcestershire sauce
  A few tablespoons water
  You will also need: Dutch oven; string if making rolled roast

For Dutch Oven Cooking: Prepare campfire; preheat Dutch oven lid in coals. Remove all fat and connective tissue from venison roast. Season roast with salt and pepper to taste. Squeeze juice from halved lemon all over roast. (If you're using a chuck roast or other cut that will be rolled, flatten meat and pound to even thickness throughout. Season with salt and pepper and squeeze lemon juice over the flat meat, then roll and tie in several places.)

Place several slices of bacon in bottom of Dutch oven. Place roast on top of bacon. Arrange onion and lemon slices around roast; sprinkle Worcestershire sauce over all. Place a few more slices of bacon on top of the roast, tucking remaining bacon around the roast. Place preheated lid on Dutch oven. Position Dutch oven over small bed of coals; place additional hot coals on top of lid. Bake for 1 hour, replenishing coals as necessary. Check after the hour and add water if necessary to prevent burning. Re-cover and bake for 30 to 60 minutes longer, or until roast is tender; replenish coals as necessary. Remove roast from Dutch oven and let sit for 10 to 15 minutes before carving to let juices distribute evenly.

For Camp or Home Cooking in an Oven: Heat oven to 325°F. Prepare roast as directed above, placing into Dutch oven or casserole. Bake for 2 to 2 1/2 hours, checking occasionally and adding water as necessary. If using a meat thermometer, remove when the center of the roast is at 125°F for rare, or 130° to 135°F for medium-rare. As the roast sits, it will continue to cook and the temperature will rise another 5 degrees or so.

STREAMSIDE SALMON 'N' SPUDS: p. 21

CHEDDAR BISCUITS: p. 28

SKILLET BREAD: p. 29

CATFISH HOAGIES: p. 35

69
MIDDAY TROUT DELIGHT: p. 44

GRILLED CAMP VEGGIES: p. 47

BARBECUED MALLARD DUCK BREASTS À L'ORANGE: p. 51

VENISON FILET with MORELS: p. 62

RAINBOW TROUT and MUSHROOMS IN FOIL: p. 84

PIKE CRISPY FINGERS: p. 93

COUNTRY CRAWFISH BOIL: p. 94

76

BAKED TROUT with WILD RICE STUFFING: p. 100

BILL'S NO-FAIL SALMON SAUTÉ: p. 105

CAMPFIRE STEW: p. 108

CINNAMON-RAISIN-NUT TWISTS: p. 115

80
WILD MINT ICED TEA: p. 121

Fish Recipes

TROUT-STUFFED CORN HUSKS

On a trip to Saskatchewan, Canada, I learned that cooks there sometimes wrap fish with a native grass before putting it on the coals to cook. When I returned home to New York, I tried a variation of this technique, using corn husks (since the area around my home area in Warwick is dotted with so many cornfields). The corn husks truly add a unique flavor and aroma to this dish.

Serves: 4
Cooking Time: 30 to 60 minutes

- 4 ears fresh corn with husks intact
- 4 whole rainbow or brook trout (about 8 oz. each), gutted and gilled
  Salt and pepper
- 1/4 cup butter (half of a stick)
  You will also need: String; aluminum foil or grill grate

For Cooking Over Coals: Prepare campfire or grill. Gently peel husks off corn, leaving silk attached to corn cob and keeping peeled husks as intact as possible; cut each cob away from the husks at the base. If you are cooking without a grill grate, wrap each peeled ear of corn in foil; set aside.

Cut 8 pieces of string that are about 6 inches long; place in a bowl of water to soak for a few minutes. Season trout inside and out with salt and pepper; place 1 tablespoon butter inside each cavity. Place each trout in a corn-husk bundle; tie ends closed with wet string.

If you are using a grill grate, place unwrapped corn on grate above medium coals (if the coals are very hot, then it's a good idea to wrap the corn in foil even if using a grate); otherwise, nestle wrapped corn directly in coals. Cook for about 10 minutes, turning once or twice. Add husk-wrapped trout to grate or coals. Cook corn and trout for 10 minutes longer, turning once or twice. Unwrap 1 trout bundle and check for doneness; fish should flake easily when probed with fork. If trout is not quite done, rewrap and return to heat; continue cooking until trout flakes easily.

For Camp or Home Cooking in an Oven: Heat oven to 350°F. Husk corn and wrap trout as directed above. Boil husked corn for 5 to 7 minutes, then arrange on baking sheet with husk-wrapped trout. Bake for 10 to 12 minutes longer, or until fish flakes easily with fork; turn fish and corn halfway through cooking time.

Tips for Grilling Fish

☞ The best utensils for grilling fish are a hinged wire basket and a long metal spatula. The hinged basket will protect smaller and more delicate pieces of fish during grilling. The long metal spatula will make it easier to flip larger pieces of fillets or steaks, so you can avoid piercing them with a fork.

☞ Turn fish over just once to avoid breaking it up; partially cooked fish is more prone to breaking apart than raw fish, so it becomes more difficult to turn as it cooks.

☞ All fish should be room temperature before grilling. This will ensure more even cooking when on the grill.

☞ As with all foods, fish will continue to cook once taken off the grill. So, it is best to make sure the fish is not overdone when removing it from the grill. Underdone fish can be returned to the grill if necessary, but overcooked fish is impossible to repair. The same holds true with spices. Always season the fish after it is off the grill. It can be difficult to remedy an overseasoned piece of fish once it is done cooking!

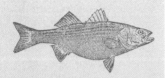

GRILL-ROASTED STRIPED BASS

The New Jersey, New York and Long Island coastlines are prime areas for striped bass. Big stripers are often caught under the Verrazano Bridge, in and around the Statue of Liberty, and even farther up the Hudson River near the Bear Mountain Bridge. Fly, live-bait and lure fishermen often catch lunkers weighing 30 to 40 pounds. This recipe can be easily prepared on the shoreline or later back at camp with fresh stripers.

Serves: 4
Cooking Time: Under 30 minutes

- 2 tablespoons olive oil, divided
- 4 cloves garlic, minced
- 2 tablespoons chopped fresh parsley
- 4 striped bass fillets (about 6 oz. each), boned but with skin on
- 1 teaspoon salt
- 1 teaspoon black pepper
- 1 lemon, sliced
  You will also need: Aluminum foil, grill grate

For Cooking Over Coals: Prepare campfire or grill. Cut 8 pieces of foil, each large enough to hold 1 fillet with plenty of excess for wrapping. Lay foil on work surface in double layers with shiny sides up (so you have 4 double-thick squares or rectangles of foil).

Drizzle about 1 teaspoon of the oil in the center of each foil square. Divide garlic and parsley evenly between foil squares. Place 1 fillet on each foil square; season with salt and pepper. Drizzle remaining oil evenly over fillets; top each fillet with lemon slices. Wrap packets by bringing together the longer sides of the foil and folding the edges together down toward the fillets (make at least 2 folds); then roll-fold ends in tightly, making 2 or 3 folds. This way, the fish cooks in its own steam.

Place foil packets on grate over hot coals. Cook for 8 to 10 minutes, depending upon thickness of fillets; turn packets halfway through. Unwrap 1 packet and check for doneness; fish should flake easily when probed with fork. If fish is not quite done, rewrap and return to heat; continue cooking until fish flakes easily. Each packet can be opened and used as a plate. The skin should not be eaten; see sidebar.

For Camp or Home Cooking in an Oven: Heat oven to 350°F. Prepare packets as directed above. Bake for 8 to 10 minutes or until fish flakes easily with fork, turning halfway through.

SALMON STEAK BARBECUE

Armed with a simple bottle of barbecue sauce, you will be a camp celebrity every time with this recipe.

<u>Serves:</u> 4
<u>Cooking Time:</u> Under 15 minutes

- 4 salmon steaks, about 1¹/₂ inches thick (8 to 10 oz. each)
  Vegetable oil for brushing grill basket
- 1 bottle barbecue sauce
  You will also need: Hinged grill basket, basting brush

<u>For Cooking Over Coals:</u> Prepare campfire or grill. Pat salmon steaks dry with paper towels. Generously oil hinged grilling basket. Coat salmon steaks with barbecue sauce and place in grill basket. Place over coals. Cook, brushing frequently with barbecue sauce, for about 5 minutes on each side or until fish flakes easily with fork.

GARLIC SALMON

I don't plan on being too close to any of my fellow campers after we've enjoyed this recipe — especially if the toothpaste is in short supply. This one is for garlic lovers only.

<u>Serves:</u> 4
<u>Cooking Time:</u> Under 30 minutes

- 1 cup Italian-style dressing, divided
- 4 skinless, boneless fillets from a 2- to 3-lb. salmon (each fillet approx. 8 oz.)
- 1 onion, sliced
- 4 cloves garlic, minced
  You will also need: Aluminum foil, grill grate

<u>For Cooking Over Coals:</u> Prepare campfire or grill. Cut 4 pieces of foil, each large enough to hold half of the salmon with plenty of excess for wrapping. Lay foil on work surface in double layers with shiny sides up (so you have 2 double-thick rectangles or squares of foil).

Drizzle about 1 teaspoon of the dressing in the center of each foil rectangle. Place fillets in center of each foil rectangle. Top each fillet with onion and garlic. Fold up edges of foil slightly to form a rim, then pour remaining dressing evenly over fillets. Wrap packets by bringing together the longer sides of the foil and folding the edges together down toward the fillets (make at least 2 folds); then roll-fold ends in tightly, making 2 or 3 folds. This way, the fish cooks in its own steam.

Place foil packets on grate over hot coals. Cook for 10 to 15 minutes, depending upon thickness of fillets; turn packets halfway through. Unwrap 1 packet and check for doneness; fish should flake easily when probed with fork. If fish is not quite done, rewrap and return to heat; continue cooking until fish flakes easily.

<u>For Camp or Home Cooking in an Oven:</u> Heat oven to 350°F. Prepare packets as directed above. Bake for 10 to 15 minutes or until fish flakes easily with fork, turning halfway through.

Marinades & Sauces

☞ Most fish require only a short period of time for marinating. The longer fish marinates, the more chance that the fish will start to cook from the acidic ingredients of the marinade.

☞ To save time, sauces can be prepared a day or two ahead; keep cool, and reheat gently just before serving.

The Lowdown on Lemons & Limes

☞ To get the most juice from your lemons or limes, roll them gently but firmly on a hard surface while pressing down with the palm of your hand before cutting them.

RAINBOW TROUT and MUSHROOMS IN FOIL

While fishing on the Wyoming ranch of Senator Bill Turner a number of years ago, we spent an afternoon fly fishing for rainbow and cutthroat trout. While we returned 90 percent of what we caught, I did keep a few to prepare along the shoreline later that evening while others fished for larger trout along the Snake River.

Serves: 4
Cooking Time: Under 30 minutes

1/2 cup all-purpose flour	12 oz. fresh mushrooms, sliced
Salt and pepper	2 tablespoons minced fresh parsley
2 lbs. rainbow trout fillets	You will also need: Aluminum foil, grill grate (optional)
1/2 cup butter (1 stick), divided	
1 cup chopped onion	

For Cooking Over Coals: Prepare grill or campfire. Season flour with salt and pepper to taste. Coat trout fillets with seasoned flour; set aside. In medium skillet over medium heat, melt 1 tablespoon of the butter and sauté onion until translucent. Add mushrooms and cook for 5 to 7 minutes longer. Stir in parsley and cook for about a minute. Remove from heat and set aside.

Cut 8 pieces of foil, each large enough to hold one-quarter of the fillets with plenty of excess for wrapping. Lay foil on work surface in double layers with shiny sides up (so you have 4 double-thick squares or rectangles of foil).

In small pan, melt remaining 3 tablespoons butter over medium heat. Drizzle a bit of melted butter on the center of each foil square, reserving half of the butter for the final step. Divide mushroom mixture evenly between 4 foil squares, piling mixture in center. Top with one-quarter of the trout fillets. Drizzle remaining melted butter on top of the fillets. Wrap packets by bringing together the longer sides of the foil and folding the edges together down toward the fillets (make at least 2 folds); then roll-fold ends in tightly, making 2 or 3 folds. This way the steam from the mushroom mixture will remain inside the foil packet, cooking the fish.

If coals are still flaming, place packets on grill grate above coals; otherwise, nestle packets directly in coals. Cook for about 15 minutes, turning once or twice. Unwrap 1 packet and check for doneness; fish should flake easily. If trout is not quite done, rewrap and return to heat; continue cooking until trout flakes easily with fork. Each packet can be opened and used as a plate.

For Camp or Home Cooking in an Oven: Heat oven to 350°F. Prepare trout packets as directed above. Bake for 15 to 20 minutes, or until fish flakes easily with fork; turn packets halfway through baking time.

STUFFED BAKED PIKE

When no one wants to eat hot dogs on a stick anymore, or if you brought too many hot dogs to camp, try this unique and tasty way to use them. They impart a nice flavor to the stuffing and the fish as well.

Serves: 8 to 10
Cooking Time: 30 to 60 minutes

4- to 5-lb. northern pike, gutted, tail and head removed

3 to 4 tablespoons butter, softened

3/4 lb. hot dogs, chopped

11/2 cups slightly crushed croutons

1/4 cup chopped onion

1/4 cup vegetable oil

1/2 teaspoon crumbled dried thyme
   Salt and pepper

6 slices bacon
   You will also need: Dutch oven, aluminum foil, toothpicks

For Dutch Oven Cooking: Prepare campfire; preheat Dutch oven lid in coals. Line inside bottom of Dutch oven with foil. Rinse and wipe cavity of northern pike; blot dry with paper towels. Coat cavity with butter. In mixing bowl, combine hot dogs, croutons, onion, oil, thyme, and salt and pepper to taste; mix well. Pack hot-dog mixture into cavity; close with toothpicks. Wrap bacon around stuffed pike, then place pike into Dutch oven. Place preheated lid on Dutch oven. Position Dutch oven over small bed of coals; place additional hot coals on top of lid. Bake for about 30 minutes, or until fish flakes easily with fork.

For Camp or Home Cooking in an Oven: Heat oven to 350°F. Prepare pike as directed above. Place stuffed pike on baking sheet. Bake for about 30 minutes, or until fish flakes easily with fork.

BAKED PIKE 'N' POTATOES

If you or your fellow campers enjoy casserole-type meals, plan to try this recipe on your next outing. It's simple and loaded with flavor. If muskellunge finds its way to your table, it's delicious in this dish.

Serves: 4
Cooking Time: 30 to 60 minutes

2 tablespoons butter

6 slices bacon, chopped

2 lbs. boneless, skinless northern pike fillets, cut into 1-inch pieces

1 large onion, chopped

4 large potatoes, sliced about 1/8 inch thick
   Salt and pepper
   Water
   You will also need: Dutch oven

For Dutch Oven Cooking: Prepare campfire; preheat Dutch oven lid in coals. Rub butter on the inside bottom and about 2 inches up the sides of the Dutch oven. Sprinkle half of the bacon into Dutch oven. Layer half of the pike, half of the onion and half of the potatoes over the bacon. Repeat layers with remaining ingredients. Season top layer with salt and pepper. Add enough water to come just to the top layer of potatoes. Place preheated lid on Dutch oven. Position Dutch oven over small bed of coals; place additional hot coals on top of lid. Bake for 35 to 40 minutes, or until fish flakes easily with fork and potatoes are tender.

For Camp or Home Cooking in an Oven: Heat oven to 350°F. Prepare as directed above, using a casserole dish in place of the Dutch oven. Cover casserole with lid or foil. Bake for 35 to 40 minutes, or until fish flakes easily with fork and potatoes are tender.

PARMESAN BAKED PERCH

For those who want fast action and good eating, perch fishing is ideal. Yellow perch, also known as ringed perch or striped perch, is the species fished most commonly throughout the United States. It finds its home in both lakes and rivers, but is most often fished in lakes with cool, clean water and rocky or sandy bottoms. The average perch weighs about ¹/₂ pound, so it'll take a few to satisfy each camper's appetite.

Serves: 6
Cooking Time: Under 30 minutes

1 cup seasoned bread crumbs
2 tablespoons grated Parmesan cheese
1 can (14 oz.) condensed milk

12 boneless, skinless perch fillets (2 to 3 oz. each)
Lemon wedges for serving, optional
You will also need: Dutch oven, aluminum foil

For Dutch Oven Cooking: Prepare campfire; preheat Dutch oven lid in coals. Line inside bottom of Dutch oven with foil. In flat dish or plastic food-storage bag, combine bread crumbs and Parmesan cheese; mix well. Pour milk into wide dish. Dip fillets in milk, then coat with crumb mixture. Arrange fillets on foil. Place preheated lid on Dutch oven. Position Dutch oven over small bed of coals; place additional hot coals on top of lid. Bake for about 30 minutes, or until fish flakes easily with fork. Serve with lemon wedges.

For Camp or Home Cooking in an Oven: Heat oven to 350°F. Spray baking sheet with nonstick spray (if you prefer, you can line the baking sheet with foil, then spray the foil). Coat fish as directed above, arranging on baking sheet. Bake for 25 to 30 minutes, or until fish flakes easily with fork. Serve with lemon wedges.

CATFISH NOODLE BAKE

Here's a charming way to prepare the flesh of one of the most underrated fish in America — the ugly, but delicious catfish. This recipe will tickle your whiskers!

Serves: 6 to 8
Cooking Time: Under 30 minutes

1 cup cornmeal
5 or 6 catfish (1 to 1¹/₂ lbs. each),
   skinned and filleted
6 slices bacon

¹/₄ cup butter (half of a stick), divided
2 tablespoons vegetable oil
3 to 4 cups cooked noodles
You will also need: Dutch oven

For Dutch Oven Cooking: Prepare campfire; preheat Dutch oven lid in coals. Place cornmeal in plastic food-storage bag. Add catfish fillets, 2 at a time, and shake to coat; set aside. In Dutch oven, fry bacon over medium heat until crisp; remove and set aside. Add half of the butter and the oil to drippings in Dutch oven. When fat mixture is hot, add catfish fillets and fry until golden. Transfer catfish fillets to plate. Drain off all but a thin layer of fat from Dutch oven. Add noodles to Dutch oven; dot with remaining butter. Lay catfish fillets on top of noodles. Top each fillet with 1 slice bacon. Place preheated lid on Dutch oven. Position Dutch oven over small bed of coals; place additional hot coals on top of lid. Bake until heated through, about 15 minutes.

WALLEYE BAKE FORESTIERE

In my mind, the only competition that walleye have for eating quality is the saltwater black fish or tautog. The flesh from both of these bottom-dwelling, hard-fighting fish is simply scrumptious.

Serves: 4 to 6

Cooking Time: 30 to 60 minutes

1/4 cup butter (half of a stick), divided

  4 large boneless, skinless walleye fillets (8 to 10 oz. each)

  1 can (10³/4 oz.) condensed cream of mushroom soup

1/2 cup white wine

1/2 cup milk

  1 can (6 oz.) mushroom pieces, drained

1/4 teaspoon pepper

1/8 teaspoon garlic powder

1/8 teaspoon salt

  1 tablespoon minced fresh parsley

    You will also need: Dutch oven

For Dutch Oven Cooking: Prepare campfire; preheat Dutch oven lid in coals. Grease inside bottom of Dutch oven with about half of the butter. Arrange walleye fillets on bottom. In small bowl, blend together soup, wine, milk, mushrooms, pepper, garlic powder and salt. Pour over fish. Cut remaining butter into bits and scatter them over fish; sprinkle parsley over all. Place preheated lid on Dutch oven. Position Dutch oven over small bed of coals; place additional hot coals on top of lid. Bake for about 30 minutes, or until fish flakes easily with fork.

For Camp or Home Cooking in an Oven: Heat oven to 350°F. Grease a 9 x 11 x 2-inch glass baking dish with about half of the butter. Arrange walleye fillets in dish. In small bowl, blend together soup, wine, milk, mushrooms, pepper, garlic powder and salt. Pour over fish. Cut remaining butter into bits and scatter them over fish; sprinkle parsley over all. Bake for 25 to 35 minutes, or until fish flakes easily with fork.

Packing Tips

☞ *Some grocery-store items like macaroni and cheese come in larger quantities; they can be portioned out at home and packed in smaller quantities to suit your group.*

☞ *A company that sells products for easy, quick and dry storage of food and other camping items:*

FoodSaver/Tilia, Inc.
P. O. Box 194530
San Francisco, CA
94119-4530
415-543-9136
www.tilia.com

(My favorite. This product is quick, reliable and well worth the investment. No more freezer burn for fish, game or venison. You can also vacuum-seal batteries, matches, maps and film on water-bound trips.)

WALLEYE in CREAMY BACON-MUSHROOM SAUCE

Peter introduced me to a variation of this recipe after returning from Canada years ago. I fine-tuned it to the recipe below. We have enjoyed this ever since; it's a great camp recipe.

Bacon Drippings at Camp

☞ *It is important to always remember to take out from the campsite all that we bring in. Frequently, some of the more annoying wastes are leftover liquids from cooking. If improperly cared for, these liquids can attract pests (both large, small and the biting kind) to the campsite or cabin. One of the more common leftovers from a campsite meal is bacon grease — a real bear attractant. Think ahead by storing it in an airtight can. This will prevent unwanted guests and give you something to cook with later in the day.*

Serves: 8
Cooking Time: 30 to 60 minutes

    2 cups all-purpose flour
       Salt and pepper
 1/4 lb. bacon (8 to 10 slices)
    2 onions, chopped
    4 lbs. boneless, skinless walleye fillets
       Vegetable oil
    2 cans (10³/4 oz. each) condensed cream of mushroom soup
    1 cup water, approx.
       You will also need: Dutch oven

For Dutch Oven Cooking: Prepare campfire; preheat Dutch oven lid in coals. Place flour in large plastic food-storage bag; add salt and pepper to taste and shake well to mix. Set aside. In Dutch oven, fry bacon over medium heat until crisp; remove and set aside. Add onions to drippings in Dutch oven. Cook over medium heat, stirring frequently, until softened. Transfer onions to dish; set aside.

Dredge walleye fillets in seasoned flour, shaking off excess. Heat about 1/4 inch of cooking oil in Dutch oven over medium-high heat. Fry walleye fillets in batches until golden; they don't have to be completely cooked at this point, just nicely colored. Transfer fried fillets to plate while you fry remaining fillets. When all fillets have been fried, drain off remaining oil. Return fried fillets to Dutch oven in layers. In mixing bowl, blend together the mushroom soup and 1 can of water. Crumble bacon into soup mixture, add cooked onion and stir well to mix. Pour soup mixture over layered fish fillets. Place preheated lid on Dutch oven. Position Dutch oven over small bed of coals; place additional hot coals on top of lid. Bake for 30 to 40 minutes; fish should flake easily with fork.

For Camp or Home Cooking in an Oven: Heat oven to 350°F. Fry walleye as directed above, layering pieces in large casserole dish. Pour soup mixture over layered fish fillets. Cover and bake for 30 to 40 minutes, or until fish flakes easily with fork.

WALLEYE in ALE

The most difficult thing about this recipe is making sure that your fellow campers leave enough beer in the cooler to prepare this dish! When I fix this on very hot summer days, I've learned to hide a couple of cans of suds ... one cup for the recipe and a can-and-a-half for me. A cold brew and walleye — does it get any better?!

Serves: 2
Cooking Time: 30 to 60 minutes

2 boneless, skinless walleye fillets (about 8 oz. each)
1 teaspoon salt
1/4 teaspoon pepper
   Paprika
2 tablespoons minced onion

3 tablespoons butter
2 tablespoons all-purpose flour
1 cup beer, room temperature
1 tablespoon brown sugar
1 tablespoon lemon juice

For Stovetop or Surface Cooking: Season walleye filets with salt, pepper, and paprika to taste; set aside. In skillet over medium heat, sauté onion in butter until tender. When onion is tender, sprinkle flour into skillet, stirring constantly; stir well to blend. Continue cooking until flour begins to brown; do not let it burn. Add beer in a thin stream, stirring constantly; continue stirring until thoroughly mixed. Heat to a gentle boil, stirring constantly. Stir in the brown sugar. Add seasoned walleye fillets to the skillet. Cover and simmer for 20 to 25 minutes, or until fish flakes easily with fork. Transfer fillets to serving plates. Drizzle lemon juice over fillets; top with beer sauce.

POACHED SALMON STEAKS

This is a recipe not only for mushroom lovers, but also for those who want a change of pace from grilling or frying fish. It is a wonderful summer recipe that is light and tasty.

Serves: 4
Cooking Time: 30 to 60 minutes

1 quart chicken broth
12 button mushrooms, thinly sliced
2 wild onions or scallions, finely chopped
1 green bell pepper, cored and finely chopped

4 salmon steaks, 1 inch thick (8 to 10 oz. each)
1 teaspoon salt
1/4 teaspoon pepper

For Stovetop or Surface Cooking: In large skillet or Dutch oven, heat chicken broth to simmering. Add mushrooms, onions and green pepper. Let simmer for 10 minutes. Transfer broth and vegetables to a container. Place salmon steaks in bottom of the skillet or Dutch oven and season with salt and pepper. Pour vegetables and enough of the hot broth on top of the steaks to just cover; keep remaining broth warm. Simmer gently (do not boil) for 15 to 20 minutes, or until fish flakes easily with fork; add additional warm broth as necessary during cooking to keep steaks covered.

SAVORY POACHED BROOKIES

Native brook trout are found in the small creeks and streams that abound in my home state of New York. The large ones caught there are about 12 inches, and at this size their flesh is quite delectable. No matter where I go, though, I've noticed that brook trout are highly prized table fare in any camp I've visited.

Serves: 4
Cooking Time: Under 30 minutes

4 thick slices bacon, cut in half	Water
4 brook trout (each 1/2 lb. or less), gutted and gilled	1/2 cup butter (1 stick)
	4 medium onions, chopped

For Stovetop or Surface Cooking: In skillet or Dutch oven, fry bacon over medium heat until crisp; remove and set aside. Drain and discard bacon drippings. Arrange trout in same pan in single layer; add water to almost cover fish. Cover and heat to a full simmer; the water needs to be just under the boiling point to cook the fish properly, but should not boil. Simmer for about 10 minutes.

Meanwhile, in another skillet, melt butter over medium heat and sauté onion until translucent. Crumble in the bacon and stir to combine. Check the trout; they should be close to done but still a bit undercooked. When trout are at this stage, pour off poaching liquid. Spread onion mixture over trout. Cover and cook over low heat for about 2 minutes longer, to let onion flavor seep into trout.

WALLEYE CORDON BLEU

The aroma of this dish while cooking is beguiling, and its flavor is beyond description. Note to the diet-conscious: this dish is very rich and also high in sodium, but it is so delicious that it's well worth falling off the wagon ... just this once!

Serves: 2
Cooking Time: Under 30 minutes

4 boneless, skinless walleye fillets, no more than 1/2 inch thick (about 4 oz. each)	1 can (10 3/4 oz.) condensed cream of celery soup
4 slices deli ham (3/4 oz. each)	2 tablespoons chopped scallions
4 slices Swiss cheese (3/4 oz. each)	1 1/2 cups water, approx.
	You will also need: Toothpicks

For Stovetop or Surface Cooking: Top each fish fillet with a slice each of ham and cheese. Roll up and secure with toothpick. In skillet or Dutch oven, combine soup, scallions and a soup-can of water; stir to blend. Heat to boiling over medium heat, stirring occasionally. Add rolled-up fish fillets, spooning some of the soup mixture over each roll. Cover skillet and cook for 8 to 10 minutes, basting rolls with soup mixture every few minutes. Fish will flake easily when done.

Backpack Surprise

The first time I cooked with foil was years ago, when Peter and I were trout fishing along one of the pristine mountain rivers of Montana's Rocky Mountains near Flathead Lake. We had hiked far up into the thick pine forest and were in awe of Mother Nature's surrounding beauty. At the same time, however, we were having a blast catching trout with nearly every cast! While we released most of what we caught, we kept a few as it neared lunchtime. Peter and I had only our backpacks with us, and I was thinking about a simple

continued on page 91

MIDWEST LOBSTER

Friends from the Midwest tell me that the northern pike is often referred to as the "lobster of the Midwest." It's a fitting name; northern pike prepared this way is as delicious as its more expensive namesake.

<u>Serves:</u> 8 to 10
<u>Cooking Time:</u> Under 30 minutes

- 3 quarts water
- 4 to 5 lbs. skinless northern pike fillets, "Y" bones removed
- 3 cups butter (6 sticks)
- 2 teaspoons garlic powder
  Salt and pepper

<u>For Stovetop or Surface Cooking:</u> In large pot or Dutch oven, heat water to boiling over high heat. Cut fish into 2-inch chunks. Add chunks to boiling water. When water returns to boiling, begin timing; cook for about 6 minutes, or until fish is tender. (If cooked too long, the chunks will begin to fall apart.) While fish is boiling, melt butter in separate saucepan over medium heat. Stir garlic powder into melted butter. Remove from heat but keep warm. When fish is done, gently remove from boiling water; season to taste with salt and pepper. Serve fish with melted butter.

PERCH PANFRY

Greenwood Lake lies half in New Jersey and half in New York, not far from our home. It is renowned for its largemouth bass and lake trout fishing. Often over-looked, however, is the lake's large population of perch. On any given early-morning or late-evening fishing adventure, we can catch enough perch to prepare this meal several times during the month.

<u>Serves:</u> 4
<u>Cooking Time:</u> Under 15 minutes

- 1 cup all-purpose flour
  Salt and pepper
- 2 eggs
- 2 teaspoons milk

- 12 medium-sized boneless, skinless perch fillets (about 4 oz. each)
- 1 cup cornmeal or crushed cracker crumbs
- 1/2 cup vegetable oil, approx.

<u>For Stovetop or Surface Cooking:</u> Place flour in large plastic food-storage bag; add salt and pepper to taste and shake well to mix. In bowl or flat dish, beat together eggs and milk. Flour each perch fillet, dip into egg mixture, then coat with corn-meal; transfer to plate in a single layer as each is coated. Let fillets sit for about 5 minutes at room temperature. Heat about 1/4 inch of cooking oil in large skillet or Dutch oven over medium-high heat. Panfry fillets for 3 to 4 minutes each side.

continued from page 90

meal of trout on a stick. But as usual, Peter surprised me. Out from his backpack he pulled an onion, a carrot, a shaker filled with a mixture of salt/pepper/garlic powder and several pieces of neatly folded heavy-duty aluminum foil. We gutted the fish, sliced the onion, and chopped the carrots. Peter sprinkled the inside of the trout's cavity with the seasoning. We placed the carrots on the foil, then added the seasoned trout and topped it with the onions. I wrapped up the fish and sealed it as if the foil were butcher paper, then wrapped the sealed package with another piece of foil. As soon as the fire had burned down to glowing coals, we tossed the packages in, and soon were enjoying the best-tasting trout we ever shared over a campfire!

Frying & Seasoning Tips

☞ If your camp kitchen has some available, a little bit of cornstarch mixed with flour for coating fish, vegetables or game will produce a crisper coating when fried.

☞ Here's a camp-cooking tip: Many recipes at camp call for seasoning with salt and pepper, or seasoning some flour before coating an item. I find it convenient to prepack a plastic salt/pepper shaker with a mixture of salt and pepper before leaving on a trip. This way I have three shakers: one with salt, one with pepper and one with a blend of the two. It makes seasoning food items much easier.

FRIED CATFISH

While hunting turkey in Alabama one year, I took a gobbler early on and had some extra time. I asked my guide what type of fishing was available. In a slow, southern drawl he said, "Gar and whiskers." "Whiskers?" I asked. He said, "Y'all Yankees call them catfish." With that, he led me to a river where I caught a couple of the largest catfish that I've ever had the pleasure of fighting. I also caught numerous 2- and 3-pounders — many more than I could keep. But I did keep enough to make this recipe at the camp shack we were staying in that evening.

<u>Serves:</u> 4 to 6
<u>Cooking Time:</u> Under 30 minutes

4 whole small catfish (about 2 lbs. each), gutted and skinned	1/2 lb. bacon
1/2 teaspoon salt	1/2 cup milk
1/4 teaspoon pepper	1/2 cup cornmeal
	Lemon wedges for serving, optional

<u>*For Stovetop or Surface Cooking:*</u> Sprinkle insides of catfish with salt and pepper. In large skillet or Dutch oven, fry bacon over medium heat until crisp; remove and set aside. While bacon is cooking, dip fish into milk, then coat with cornmeal. Let sit for a few minutes. After bacon has been removed, cook catfish in bacon drippings for 4 to 5 minutes on each side. The fish is done when it flakes easily with a fork. Crumble bacon and sprinkle over catfish. Serve with lemon wedges.

SAUTÉED TROUT <u>with</u> WILD ONIONS

You can make trout in dozens of different ways, but no preparation has been used more than sautéed trout. And why not? It's quick, it's easy and it makes my mouth water even as I type this. No wonder this long-lasting method of cooking is used by so many outdoorsmen and women.

<u>Serves:</u> 4
<u>Cooking Time:</u> Under 15 minutes

1 cup all-purpose flour	2 tablespoons butter
Salt and pepper	8 to 10 wild onions, thinly sliced (including green tops)
2 whole trout (about 2 lbs. each), gutted and gilled	Juice from 1 lemon

<u>*For Stovetop or Surface Cooking:*</u> Place flour in large plastic food-storage bag; add salt and pepper to taste and shake well to mix. Coat trout with seasoned flour, shaking off any excess. In large skillet or Dutch oven, melt butter over medium heat until sizzling. Add trout and cook until golden brown on both sides. Push browned trout to a cooler side of the skillet. Add onions and lemon juice. Sauté for a few minutes, then spoon juices over trout and check for doneness. The trout is done when it flakes easily with a fork; continue cooking a minute or 2 longer if necessary.

PIKE CRISPY FINGERS

These tasty morsels will be a favorite in any camp. They're not only fun to make, but they're also a fun finger food to eat as well.

<u>Serves:</u> 4 to 6
<u>Cooking Time:</u> Under 15 minutes

  2 to 3 lbs. boneless, skinless pike fillets
  1 cup cornmeal
  1 cup all-purpose flour
  1 or 2 eggs
 1/4 cup butter (half of a stick), approx.
 1/4 cup vegetable oil, approx.
     Salt and pepper

<u>For Stovetop or Surface Cooking:</u> Cut pike fillets into "fingers" about 2 inches long by 1 inch wide. Combine cornmeal and flour in shallow dish. Beat 1 egg in another dish. Dip each finger into egg, then coat with cornmeal mixture. (If you run out of egg before all fish has been coated, also use the second egg.) In large skillet or Dutch oven, melt equal parts of butter and oil to come about 1/4 inch up the sides. Fry fingers until crispy, 2 to 3 minutes, turning to cook all sides. Salt and pepper to taste before serving.

BEER BATTER PERCH

There is always trouble brewing when I prepare this recipe, especially in camps that we pitch during the summer. You've got it — keeping the beer from being consumed by the anglers (mostly the guys) is always challenging, but once you've learned how to protect the cook's stash, this is always a winner.

<u>Serves:</u> 4
<u>Cooking Time:</u> Under 15 minutes

 12 boneless, skinless perch fillets
     (about 4 oz. each)
  1 teaspoon salt
 1/2 teaspoon pepper

 1 1/2 cups pancake mix
  1 can (12 oz.) beer
  1 egg
     Vegetable oil

<u>For Stovetop or Surface Cooking:</u> Cut perch into 3-inch strips; season with salt and pepper. In mixing bowl, combine pancake mix, beer and egg; beat with whisk, egg beater or fork until smooth. In deep skillet or Dutch oven, heat 2 to 3 inches oil over medium-high heat. Test the oil by dropping a bit of batter into the skillet; when the oil is hot enough the batter will bubble and begin to cook instantly. Dip perch strips into batter, letting excess drip off. Cook strips, a few at a time, until golden brown on all sides, 3 to 4 minutes. Drain on paper towel–lined plate.

Seasonings & More

☞ *There are a few companies that offer excellent seasonings and marinades for wild game and fish. Here are my favorites:*

Shore Lunch
Sportsman's Recipes inc.
8565 Highway 65 NE
Blaine, MN 55434
800-473-4557
www.shorelunch.com

(My favorite. With over 30 years' experience in the outdoor cooking industry, they offer breading and batter mixes, spices and rubs, marinades, and cooking oil.)

Totally Wild Seasonings
10344 County Road,
X-61
Wapello, IA 52653
319-523-4428
www.totallywild
seasonings.com

(All-purpose breading, shaker seasonings, jerky seasonings, fish and seafood boil mixes, cajun and barbecue seasonings and smoking cures and mixes.)

COUNTRY CRAWFISH BOIL

Who would expect to be eating crawfish while on a deer hunting trip? This was the surprise both Peter and I enjoyed several years ago while taping a segment in Louisiana for our television program. We had just returned from the afternoon's post and were a bit tired from the shoot and the cool, damp weather that chilled us to the bone. The camp chef, Bubba (that really was his name), served this scrumptious meal that warmed us right up. Since then, when crawfish are available at our local market, I prepare this at home.

Serves: 10 to 12
Cooking Time: 30 to 60 minutes

8 potatoes, cut into 1-inch chunks	Water
3 onions, cut into 1-inch chunks	5 lbs. crawfish (see sidebar at left)
3 stalks celery, cut into 1-inch chunks	3 lbs. kielbasa, cut into 1-inch chunks
4 garlic cloves, peeled and crushed	5 ears fresh corn, husked and cut into 2-inch wheels
1/4 cup Old Bay seasoning	
1 teaspoon cayenne pepper	

For Stovetop or Surface Cooking: In large Dutch oven or stockpot combine potatoes, onions, celery, garlic, Old Bay, and cayenne. Add water to come 2 to 3 inches above the ingredients. Cover and heat to boiling over high heat. Boil for 15 minutes, or until potatoes are tender.

Add crawfish, kielbasa and corn; mix thoroughly. Return to boiling, then let boil for about 2 minutes. Remove from heat and let stand for about 5 minutes. Drain and serve immediately on large platters.

BOILED CRAWFISH

The key to a good flavor with this recipe is to be sure that your crawfish were taken from fast-moving waters. You and the kids can collect a potfull in short order in shin-deep water. Simply have the kids turn some rocks while you stand a few feet ahead of them, scooping up escaping crawfish. They'll brighten any camp — anytime.

Serves: 4
Cooking Time: Under 15 minutes

6 to 8 quarts water	2 tablespoons vinegar
2 lbs. crawfish (see sidebar at left)	1 lb. butter, melted

For Stovetop or Surface Cooking: Into large Dutch oven or stockpot, pour enough water to accommodate the crawfish without overcrowding them. Heat to a rolling boil over high heat. Add vinegar to boiling water. Slowly add crawfish to boiling water; they need to be added slowly so that the water continues to boil. Cook them no longer than 3 to 5 minutes. Drain and serve with melted butter.

Crawfish

☞ *If you have just caught some fresh crawfish, make sure that you rinse and scrub them several times before cooking. If time permits, allow them to soak overnight in cool running water, then give them one final rinse before cooking. Most important, the crawfish must still be alive when you cook them. Any dead or limp ones must be discarded.*

GRILLED LOBSTER

I spent most of my teen summers in Boothbay Harbor, Maine. During this time I learned about fishing for mackerel and flounder. I also ate some very fresh lobster. Whenever summer guests would come to visit us, "the kids" were sent out on the 16-foot Mini to bring back a huge stockpot of fresh seawater with a little bit of seaweed or kelp, critical ingredients for boiling up a mess of fresh lobster. Some of the older family members were assigned a mission of meeting with a lobsterman on his way back to port and negotiating for some of the freshest lobsters on board. In the end, the team effort always made for a wonderful evening of preparing and eating these delectable crustaceans. Here's a great summertime recipe that is easy to prepare at camp.

Serves: 4
Cooking Time: 30 to 60 minutes

- 4 quarts water, plus a big container of ice water
- 1/4 cup sea salt
- 4 live lobsters
- 1 cup butter (2 sticks)
- 1/2 cup finely chopped shallots (if you don't have shallots at camp, garlic will do)
- 1 teaspoon fresh lemon juice
  You will also need: Grill grate

For Cooking Over Coals: In stockpot or large Dutch oven, combine 4 quarts water and the salt, stirring to dissolve salt. Or, if fresh seawater is available, use that! Heat water to boiling over high heat*. Place lobsters into the boiling water. Return to boiling and cook for 3 to 4 minutes, until lobster shells turn red. Remove lobsters from boiling water and plunge into ice water to stop the cooking. This can be done ahead of the final cooking time if need be; just be sure to keep the lobsters cool until grilling time.

Prepare grill or campfire. In small skillet, melt butter over low heat. Add shallots and sauté until translucent. Add lemon juice and heat through. Remove from heat. Divide into 2 portions: half for basting the lobster and the other half for dipping sauce.

Cut lobsters in half lengthwise; remove intestines and liver. Position grate 4 to 6 inches over coals. Place lobster halves on grate, shell side down; brush with seasoned butter mixture. Cook for about 8 minutes, or until the lobster meat is solid white, turning once. Serve with remaining heated seasoned butter.

*Note: The preliminary cooking of the lobsters can be done over a campfire or on the stovetop.

General Camping Philosophy

☞ *With millions of folks enjoying the outdoors each and every year, it is of the utmost importance that we keep our impact on the environment to a minimum. In that way, our children and our children's children will be able to enjoy the wilderness as much as we do. Do everything you can to keep your camping adventures impact-free and avoid leaving any unwanted marks on the land when you leave.*

OUTFITTERS' BEST CAMP RECIPES

My career in the outdoors has provided me the opportunity to meet some wonderful folks over the last eighteen years – and not just while taping hunting or fishing segments for our TV program or while on a magazine assignment. I have met some of the most memorable people when I was simply afield enjoying time away from work.

One such encounter happened in Alaska one fall. Peter and I stayed afield a bit too long and got turned around on the way back. Luckily, just at twilight, we came across a group of hunters who had a pitched tent on a hill above the river. Their guide invited us in for dinner, and we enjoyed a wonderfully prepared moose meal that he whipped up in what seemed like fifteen minutes. I have used that recipe many times since – always thinking of his kindness and hospitality, even though I have never seen or heard from him since.

Another friendship was kindled when Peter and I were fishing brookies in a remote part of the Adirondack Mountains on Pharaoh Lake. An unexpected and violent thunderstorm quickly swept in over the mountain behind us. We had just made it back to shore when lightning began to snap all around us. As we tried to find shelter, we heard a voice from a nearby lean-to: "Come in here. Join us for some hot coffee and something to eat." The voice belonged to a local guide, who willingly shared his food and shelter – and that wasn't all. By the end of the day, he'd shared one of his closest-kept secret recipes for fresh brook trout with me. We have fished with him many times over the years and have shared friendship and many more tasty recipes. And to think that it all stemmed from that one generous invitation!

In fact, most of my best camp recipes have come from guides, some with whom I've booked trips and others who I just happened to meet on the trail or in the field. I have included their best recipes (and my favorites!) here. I hope you enjoy eating them as much as I did when they were first prepared for me.

NORTHERN WILDLIFE VENISON POPCORN

TABA LARSON / NORTHERN WILDLIFE VENTURES,
DEBDEN, SASKATCHEWAN, CANADA

We enjoyed these camp delights when hunting elk at Northern Wildlife Ventures. Taba, one of the owner's daughters, was the camp chef and her cooking talents went way beyond her years (she was just 19 at the time). Beginning at 4 a.m. and still going long after 9 p.m., she spent each day preparing meals that were both unforgettable and delicious. This was one of her specialties.

Serves: 6 to 8
Cooking Time: Under 30 minutes

- 2   lbs. boneless venison steak (any type of venison will do)
- 2   cups all-purpose flour, seasoned with garlic powder, lemon pepper and salt
   Corn oil for frying

For Stovetop or Surface Cooking: Chop venison into 1/2-inch cubes. Be sure that all connective tissue has been removed. Toss cubes in seasoned flour and shake to remove any excess. Heat about 1/2 inch of oil in large skillet or Dutch oven over high heat. Add a few cubes and cook until nicely browned on all sides (don't try to cook too many cubes at one time, or they won't cook quickly enough). Transfer cooked cubes to paper towel–lined plate while you fry the remaining cubes. Serve warm.

Northern Wildlife Ventures is a 1,500-acre facility that offers superb hunts for trophy-class elk and whitetails in central Saskatchewan's rolling hills, forests and meadows. On a recent trip, our hunting party took a 396 7/8-class 7x8 bull elk and a 207 3/8-class whitetail buck. The ranch offers many opportunities for trophies of this caliber. Situated on lakefront property, the ranch also offers some great fishing for walleye and northern pike.

Worldwide Wilderness 888-223-2117; Northern Wildlife Ventures 306-724-4509
www.worldwidewilderness.com

Elk Antlers

☞ *Bull elk may have antlers more than 5 feet long. Those with 6 points on each antler are called royal elk; 7 points, imperial elk; and 8 points, monarchs.*

☞ *In the fall, bull elk practice fighting by aggressively rubbing their antlers on trees. These rubs announce a bull's presence to other elk. Elk rubs resemble those made by whitetails, but may be on larger trees.*

BAKED DUCK and RICE

JOE ZERKOWKSY, CHEF / NILO FARMS, BRIGHTON, ILLINOIS

Back in the early '90s, Peter and I were invited to hunt at Winchester-Olin's famed Nilo Farms. Along with several other outdoor couples, we were treated to an insightful tour of the ammunition manufacturing facility. We then headed afield for some fun and challenging pheasant, quail and duck hunting. Later, Nilo chef Joe Zerkowsky prepared some of the day's bounty and served forth the most delicious and satisfying wild game dishes. Below is one of his signature recipes, adapted for camp use.

Serves: 2 or 3
Cooking Time: 1¹/₂ to 2 hours

¹/₄ cup all-purpose flour	1 tablespoon chopped green bell pepper
Salt, pepper and paprika	2¹/₂ cups water or tomato juice
1 large or 2 medium ducks (2 to 2¹/₂ lbs. total), cut up	2 tablespoons ketchup
¹/₃ cup vegetable shortening or oil	1 teaspoon sage
³/₄ cup uncooked rice	¹/₂ teaspoon crumbled bay leaf
1 small onion, chopped	Dash of cayenne
	You will also need: Dutch oven

For Dutch Oven Cooking: Prepare campfire; preheat Dutch oven lid in coals. Place flour in large plastic food-storage bag; add salt, pepper and paprika to taste and shake well to mix. Coat duck pieces in seasoned flour, shaking off excess. In Dutch oven, heat shortening or oil over medium-high heat until hot. Add duck pieces and brown on all sides. Transfer duck pieces to warm skillet or dish; set aside and keep warm.

Add rice, onion and green pepper to drippings in Dutch oven and sauté for about 20 minutes, until lightly browned. Add water, ketchup, sage, bay leaf and cayenne. Heat to boiling; cook for 10 minutes. Return duck pieces to Dutch oven, spooning mixture over the ducks to cover them well. Place preheated lid on Dutch oven. Position Dutch oven over small bed of coals; place additional hot coals on top of lid. Bake for 1 hour, checking halfway through and adding additional cooking liquid as necessary; replenish coals as necessary during cooking.

For Camp or Home Cooking in an Oven: Heat oven to 350°F. Prepare duck and rice mixture as described above, combining in a casserole dish. Cover and bake for about 1 hour; stir and check twice during baking to see if additional liquid is needed.

With 640 acres of rolling hills and woodlands and agricultural fields, NILO Farms offers some of the country's best hunting for ring-necked pheasants, chukar partridges, and mallard ducks. Shooters can also enjoy excellent facilities for trap, crazy quail, skeet, riverside skeet, sporting clays, 5-stand and the tower. Expert guides, well-trained dogs, and firearms are also available.

Nilo Farms, Brighton, IL, 618-466-0613, Manager – Roger Green, www.nilofarms.com

PAT'S MARINATED VENISON

PAT DONOVAN / KANE LAKE OUTFITTERS, NORTHERN SASKATCHEWAN, CANADA

Pat's love of the outdoors is evident in his cooking of both wild game and fish. This is one of his favorite game recipes. The venison is moist, tender and spicy, whether cooked on a grill (as Pat prefers), or prepared in a skillet. Note that although the total preparation for this recipe takes over 2 hours, actual cooking time is under 30 minutes.

<u>Serves:</u> 3 or 4
<u>Cooking Time:</u> Over 2 hours

   1 lb. boneless venison, trimmed of all fat and connective tissue
   2 tablespoons soy sauce
   2 tablespoons extra-virgin olive oil
   1 teaspoon hot red pepper flakes
 1/2 teaspoon ginger
 1/2 teaspoon garlic powder
      You will also need: Skewers

For Cooking Over Coals: Cut venison into small strips or cubes; place in plastic container. Mix remaining ingredients together and pour over venison. Seal container and shake thoroughly. The mixture should be allowed to marinate for at least 2 hours (the longer, the better); shake the container occasionally during marinating.

Prepare grill or campfire. Thread venison cubes on skewers. Grill over hot coals until just cooked to your liking; take care not to overcook, or the meat will be dry and tough.

For Stovetop or Surface Cooking: Marinate venison as described above. When ready to cook, heat a little oil in a skillet over medium-high heat. Drain venison cubes and fry in small batches until nicely browned and cooked to your liking.

Affordable trophy hunting and excellent fishing are what you'll experience with Kane Lake Outfitters in Saskatchewan. Their fly and spinfishing for 8- to 10-pound lake trout, huge northern pike, 3- to 6-pound walleye and spectacular Arctic grayling is second to none. The lakes they fish are accessed by road, but they are so pristine, you'd swear that they're "fly-in-only"! While they've been running their fishing camps for over 18 years, their newly developed hunting program has yielded trophy results, including 400- to 500-pound bears in three colors, and moose with racks from 48 to 55 inches! Their fall hunts can be combined with their fishing, and that makes this outfit one to put on your "must visit" list.

Kane Lake Outfitters; 888-223-2117, www.kanelake.com

Moose Trivia

☞ Moose weigh 25 to 35 pounds at birth, grow to adult size in 4 to 5 years and live up to 18. A full-grown Canada bull moose weighs 1,000 to 1,400 pounds and has antlers measuring over 4 feet from tip to tip.

☞ Moose tracks measure about 6 inches long. The prints cut deeply into soft ground, accounting for many of the portage trails connecting remote, northern lakes.

☞ Moose are quite vocal, especially during the breeding season. Cows emit a long, quivering moan that ends in a coughlike "mooo-agh," which can be heard for up to 2 miles. Bulls respond with a deep, coarse grunt or bellow. Hunters imitate these sounds to call moose within shooting range.

BAKED TROUT with WILD RICE STUFFING

ANN TARDIF / WHALE RIVER LODGE, QUEBEC, CANADA

Peter and I have known Alain and Ann Tardif for nearly 18 years. On our latest hunting trip for caribou at Whale River Lodge, we spent a few days fishing for spawning lake trout. We caught enough fish to feed the 20 hunters in camp three out of the six days we were there. This recipe turned out to be a camp favorite. Note that the rice for this dish needs to be prepared in advance.

<u>Serves:</u> 4
<u>Cooking Time:</u> 30 to 60 minutes

  1 onion, chopped
  1 stalk celery, chopped
1$^{1}/_{2}$ cups chopped fresh mushrooms
  3 tablespoons margarine
$^{1}/_{2}$ cup uncooked wild rice, soaked overnight or cooked for 1 hour
$^{1}/_{4}$ teaspoon pepper
    Salt
  4 trout (1 lb. each), gutted and gilled
  2 tablespoons butter, melted
$^{1}/_{2}$ cup dry white wine
  1 tablespoon minced fresh parsley
    You will also need: Skewers

<u>For Camp or Home Cooking in an Oven:</u> Heat oven to 450°F. In skillet, sauté the onion, celery and mushrooms in margarine over medium heat. Remove from heat; stir in drained rice, pepper, and salt to taste. Wash trout; sprinkle with salt. Stuff with rice mixture. Close body cavities with thin skewers. Arrange trout in baking dish. Brush with butter; sprinkle with wine and parsley. Cover and bake until fish flakes easily with fork, 15 to 20 minutes.

Alain and Ann Tardif have been in the outfitting business for over 30 years. In addition to offering excellent caribou hunts from their Whale River and Leaf River Lodges, the Tardifs also provide superb fishing opportunities during the summer months. Their pristine camps are located in northern Quebec. Guests fly 2 hours north of Montreal by jet, then board a float plane and fly another 2$^{1}/_{2}$ hours north from there! It always amazes me how many comforts of home are found at the Tardifs' camps, even though they are so far away from anything or anyone!

Whale River Lodge; 800-463-4868, www.whaleriverlodge.com

Lakers: Fish of the North

☞ *Lake trout move into shallow water just before the fall spawning period. They spawn over a bottom of baseball- to football-sized rocks, usually at a depth of 5 to 20 feet. You can often catch numbers of shallow-water lakers by casting flashy spoons.*

☞ *Lake trout grow slowly in the frigid waters of the North. In some lakes or northern Canada, a 10-pound laker might be 20 years of age or even older. The age of a trophy lake trout may exceed 40 years.*

BOB'S "NO CLEANUP" GRILLED SALMON

BOB CINELLI / CINELLI'S SPORTFISHING, LOCKPORT, NEW YORK

When Bob cooks fish, this is his favorite recipe. After dinner, just roll up the foil and there are no pots and pans to scrub! For a guy who's as busy as Bob is, the easy cleanup makes this recipe number one on his list.

<u>Serves:</u> 2
<u>Cooking Time:</u> Under 30 minutes

2 salmon fillets (8 oz. each), boned but with skin on
2 tablespoons butter (Bob uses butter from a squeeze bottle)
    Lawry's seasoned salt, paprika, and garlic powder
2 slices red onion
    You will also need: Grill grate, aluminum foil

<u>For Cooking Over Coals:</u> Prepare campfire or grill; let coals burn down to low embers (if using a gas grill, adjust flame to low setting). Place grate over coals. Place foil on grate and poke holes to let the liquid from the salmon run through during cooking. Place fillets on foil, skin side down. Place 1 tablespoon butter on each fillet. Season with the spices to your taste. Place 1 onion slice on top of each fillet. Cook for about 20 minutes, or until fish flakes easily with fork. To serve, slide a spatula between the flesh and the skin. The cooked skin will stick to the foil, making it easy to slide the skinless salmon fillet off the grill.

When the foil has cooled, roll it up with the skin on and throw it away … no pans to clean!

> Peter and I have been fishing Lake Ontario with Captain Bob since the 1980s. He's been a guest on our television series numerous times and always provides exciting action for the viewers. There hasn't been a trip on Lake Ontario when we haven't caught football-sized brown trout, big lakers, steelhead and huge king salmon – some weighing over 30 pounds. Bob runs a tight, professional sportfishing outfit with an excellent crew. He works hard from sunup to sundown and even handles the day's-end task of cleaning and filleting your catch!
>
> Cinelli's Sportfishing, 716-433-5210

Salmon Spawning

☞ Salmon are "anadromous" fish, which means they spend most of their life at sea, then return to freshwater rivers and streams to spawn. But many species of salmon, including king, coho, sockeye and Atlantic, have been successfully stocked in many freshwater lakes.

☞ Pacific salmon die shortly after spawning; Atlantic salmon do not. Atlantic salmon are more closely related to trout, and may live to spawn two or more times.

☞ As Pacific salmon move into rivers and streams to spawn, their color changes from bright silver to reddish or brownish and finally to black.

THOROFARE DUTCH OVEN BREAKFAST

TOM "COOKIE" FARNWORTH, CHEF / HIDDEN CREEK OUTFITTERS, CODY, WYOMING

Bill Perry is the owner of Hidden Creek Outfitters. His camps are among the most scenic that I have been to in North America. The camp where we first enjoyed this recipe was nestled in a pristine valley of the Bitterroot Mountains; it took a 10-hour horseback trip into the wilderness to reach this remote camp. The only thing more alluring than the bugles from bulls echoing from canyon to canyon was the aroma continually wafting from the cook tent at each meal.

<u>Serves:</u> 4 to 6
<u>Cooking Time:</u> Under 30 minutes

1   dozen eggs
    Salt and pepper
3   tablespoons olive oil
6   potatoes, cut into 1/8-inch dice
2   medium onions, diced
3   cloves garlic, minced
3   bell peppers (one yellow, one red, one green), cored and diced
    For serving: Grated cheddar cheese, sour cream or salsa, warmed tortillas

<u>*For Stovetop or Surface Cooking:*</u> In mixing bowl, beat eggs with salt and pepper to taste; set aside. In 12-inch Dutch oven, heat oil over medium heat. Add the diced potatoes to hot oil. Cook until tender, stirring frequently. Add onions and garlic; sauté until onions are translucent. Add peppers; sauté until peppers are soft. Remove Dutch oven from heat and immediately pour beaten eggs over the vegetables. Do not stir. Cover Dutch oven and let sit for about 5 minutes, until eggs are cooked. Serve with grated cheddar cheese, and sour cream or salsa; warmed tortillas are good with this also.

Hidden Creek Outfitters runs several camps in different locations in the scenic mountains of northwestern Wyoming; some of the camps border Yellowstone National Park. Bill's success rate for elk runs incredibly high – 95 percent or perhaps even higher. He also guides for mule deer, bear, moose, sheep and mountain lion. The hunts are affordable and the guides are knowledgeable and friendly. Bill also offers summer horse-pack trips into the wilderness, where catching and releasing up to 150 cutthroat a day is not uncommon.

Hidden Creek Outfitters: 307-527-5470, www.hiddencr.com

Don't Drink the Water

☞ *Never assume that the clear-running, cold, mountain-fresh water is safe to drink. There is not anything much worse than drinking contaminated water and having stomach ailments for days to come! On the mild end, this can be annoying and slightly debilitating; on the severe end, complications from drinking contaminated water can be life threatening. Therefore, one must always presume that fresh water sources on the trail are contaminated with hurtful microorganisms. Proper steps must be taken to remove these insidious bacteria before using the water.*

continued on page 103

JOHN'S BEEF TENDERLOIN

JOHN LOFTIS / COLORADO TRAILS RANCH, DURANGO, COLORADO

Cookouts on the grill and trailside breakfasts of buttermilk pancakes are just some of the outdoor treats you'll enjoy at Colorado Trails Ranch. Your appetite never seems to wane from all the time you spend each day taking in the exhilarating mountain-fresh air and gorgeous sunshine. So, when dinnertime comes around, make sure you don't miss this recipe.

Serves: 12 to 16
Cooking Time: 1 1/2 hours

   5 to 7 lbs. beef tenderloin (elk or moose will work well, too)
1/2 cup ground black pepper, plus additional as needed
   1 lb. margarine
   2 cups Worcestershire sauce
   2 tablespoon garlic salt
      You will also need: Grill grate, basting brush, tongs

For Cooking Over Coals: Rub all sides of the tenderloin with the 1/2 cup pepper; let sit at room temperature for 1 hour. Prepare campfire or grill; when ready to cook, heat grate over prepared coals.

In saucepan, melt margarine over low heat. Stir in Worcestershire sauce, garlic salt, and pepper to taste. Place loin on grate over hot coals and baste with margarine sauce. Cook until desired doneness (120° to 125°F for medium-rare), basting with sauce throughout cooking; turn meat as needed with tongs rather than a fork, to avoid piercing holes in the meat.

> Just north of Durango, Colorado, nestled in the beautiful San Juan mountains, you'll find Colorado Trails Ranch. If you have ever dreamed of taking a vacation to a dude ranch, this is the ranch for you. Not only is there excellent western riding for both adults and children, but their fly-fishing trips are exceptional. You'll fish blue-ribbon waters renowned for the trout they harbor. While at the ranch, you can also enjoy river rafting on the Animas River, trap shooting, archery, hiking, power-tubing on Vallecito Lake, or swimming in their heated pool and hot tub. Fine accommodations and mouth-watering meals round out this truly first-class ranch.
>
> Colorado Trails Ranch; 877-711-7843

continued from page 102

One of the more common nasty microorganisms is Giardia lamblia. This microbe can be ingested and remain in your system anywhere from 7 to 10 days before wreaking havoc. While it is possible to remove Giardia from a water source by chlorinating or boiling the water, both of these methods have their drawbacks. Chlorinated water is not very tasty — although it can be partially masked by some powdered drinks. Boiling water for 5 to 10 minutes, while effective, is a waste of your fuel source. The quickest and most efficient method is to filter out the microbes. Many excellent water filters are available at outdoor stores. Since Giardia are smaller than 1 micron, make sure the filter you choose can weed out those particles and other small organisms.

READERS' BEST
CAMP RECIPES

The nicest thing about camping, whether out in the woods or at a motorhome park, is the people you meet: other outdoor enthusiasts out to have a good time afield and share some camaraderie with other outdoorsmen and women. These folks are most eager to share their outdoor adventures – and often their recipes – with others. Over the years, I have come across scores of hunters, hikers, campers, RVers, snow-mobilers and anglers with whom I have shared tablefare. Many of the meals were so good, I made sure to ask for the recipe before breaking camp.

The recipes in this chapter are from friends, relatives, readers, viewers and coworkers. They are among my favorite camp dishes. I have chosen them not only for their ease of preparation but also because they produce delicious meals that provide good nutrition – an important element for anyone who will be outdoors all day. Several recipes offer the added benefit of easy cleanup as well.

One of my all-time favorite people is Bill Hilts Jr. We have shared many excursions afield with Bill, and because of his terrific sense of humor, most of these trips have been filled with side-splitting laughter – like the day Bill and Wade Boggs tried to convince Peter to stay out on the middle of Lake Ontario even though he was green to the gills. Or, the time that Bill called the dentist, who he knew was a big fan of our television show, in the middle of the night to fix a tooth Peter had broken on a jawbreaker Bill had given him!

One of Bill's most delicious recipes is included in this section (Bill's No-Fail Salmon Sauté, page 105). It comes from Bill's days as a single man, when he and his friend, Captain Bob Cinelli (another handsome, single outdoorsman), had to fend for themselves when it came to cooking. Their meals had to be healthy and provide enough energy for them to stay on the water from sun-up until well after dusk. More important, they had to be very quick to prepare, with very little cleanup. (Some things don't change with men – single or married!) Along with Bill's delicious creation, you'll find many other recipes that will be welcome on your next camping excursion.

BILL'S NO-FAIL SALMON SAUTÉ

BILL HILTS JR., SANFORD, NEW YORK

Bill is a long-time friend and associate in the outdoor industry. As the Niagara County (New York) sportfishing coordinator, he has arranged many fishing excursions for us for our television show and for article assignments. Many of these trips along the Niagara River or the surrounding waters included shoreline lunches. Here's one of Bill's favorites.

<u>Serves:</u> 2 or 3
<u>Cooking Time:</u> Under 30 minutes

1/4 cup vegetable oil, approx.
  2 boneless, skinless salmon fillets
     (8 oz. each)
  2 cloves garlic, chopped

4 slices mozzarella cheese
  (3/4 oz. each)
1 jar (14 oz.) spaghetti sauce
1 teaspoon Italian-blend dried
  seasoning

<u>For Stovetop or Surface Cooking:</u> In large skillet, heat about 1/8 inch of oil over medium heat. When hot, add salmon fillets and garlic. Cook fillets for about 2 minutes on each side; if garlic begins to turn brown, remove it from skillet. When fish has cooked for 2 minutes on each side, lay 2 slices of cheese on each fillet. Pour spaghetti sauce over cheese-topped fish. Reduce heat to simmering and cook for about 15 minutes, or until fish flakes easily with fork. Sprinkle with Italian-blend seasoning before serving.

STREAMSIDE WILLOW TROUT

BOB LOZINSKY, SASKATOON, SASKATCHEWAN, CANADA

Bob Lozinsky is the Vice President of New Markets for one of the largest outdoor booking and travel agents in North America, World Wide Wilderness Directory. Over the years, he has not only provided us with some of the cheapest airfares and some of the most memorable hunts, he has also shared many of his delicious recipes. This is a technique he shared with us while we were hunting elk and deer at Northern Wildlife Ventures.

<u>Serves:</u> 2
<u>Cooking Time:</u> Under 30 minutes

2 fresh trout, gutted and gilled   Fresh willow branches with leaves

<u>For Cooking Over Coals:</u> Build a fire from dead wood. When coals are red and glowing, place 4 to 6 layers of leafy green branches on the fire, making a bed about 2 inches thick. Lay trout on top of the leaves. Cook for about 15 minutes on each side, depending upon the size of the trout. When fish is cooked, as you peel the head back, the spine and the remaining bones pull out freely.

Taking a Guided Hunt

☞ *Don't make the mistake of spending money on a guided hunt without first talking with several people who have been on the hunt before. And don't just settle for one or two references. For example, if an outfitter routinely takes 10 moose hunters each fall, ask to get the phone numbers of all 10. If he won't give them to you, he very well may be hiding something. A reputable outfitter can't guarantee you success, but he will always provide a good camp, experienced guides, and game animals and property that have not been overhunted.*

GARLIC VENISON CUTLETS SUPREME

CATHERINE CAMARDA, KEW GARDENS HILLS, NEW YORK

My sister-in-law, Catherine, loves to cook, and spends many hours preparing exquisite meals for herself and her husband, Joe. Her passion, however, is preparing holiday feasts for the entire family. At that time of year, we gather together to enjoy her wonderfully delicious tablefare and everyone leaves stuffed and satisfied. (Even her parrot, Rudy, can't resist Catherine's homemade treats.) One of Catherine's year-round favorites is breaded venison cutlets. This is an ideal meal to be prepared at a lodge or cabin or, as we find, when camping in an RV.

<u>Serves:</u> 4 to 6
<u>Cooking Time:</u> 30 to 60 minutes

1	cup all-purpose flour
	Salt and pepper
2	eggs
1 1/2	cups milk
1	cup Italian-seasoned bread crumbs
1/4	cup grated Parmesan cheese
2	teaspoons garlic powder
8	venison cutlets (about 4 oz. each)
1/2	cup olive oil, approx.
10	garlic cloves, crushed (not chopped)

For Stovetop or Surface Cooking: Place flour in large plastic food-storage bag; add salt and pepper to taste and shake well to mix. In bowl or flat dish, beat together eggs and milk. In another shallow dish, mix together the bread crumbs, Parmesan cheese and garlic powder. Pat cutlets dry. Flour each cutlet, dip into egg mixture, then coat with bread crumb mixture; transfer to plate in a single layer as each is coated. Let cutlets sit for about 5 minutes at room temperature.

In large skillet, heat about 1/4 inch of oil over medium-low heat. When hot, add crushed garlic cloves and cook until golden, stirring constantly. Before garlic turns brown, remove from skillet. Increase heat to medium. Add breaded cutlets in small batches. Cook until nicely browned, 2 to 3 minutes on each side. Transfer browned cutlets to a paper towel–lined plate and keep warm while you prepare the remaining cutlets, adding additional oil as necessary. Serve immediately.

Holiday Deer Hunts

☞ *In much of North America, bowhunting for whitetails is open until dark on December 31st. Because of the cold, this type of hunting isn't for everyone. But if you know how to dress properly, this time of year can be an excellent time to put venison in the freezer.*

☞ *Most late-season hunters look for standing cornfields, which are magnets for winter whitetails. These fields are especially good when deep snow covers the forest floor and deer can no longer find acorns.*

FRIED SQUIRREL LEGS

HELEN DEFREESE, WARWICK, NEW YORK

Helen has been our office assistant for many years. Her work both in and out of the office has been of great value to both Peter and me. Helen's love of the outdoors is enhanced by her family's hunting and fishing journeys that yield plenty of bounty for her to prepare. From canning, smoking, pickling, roasting and panfrying, Helen has tried it all with game. I know you'll enjoy this recipe when you bring back a game bag full of squirrels! Note: These work best with young squirrel legs, as the older ones can be a bit chewy.

Serves: 3
Cooking Time: Under 30 minutes

12 squirrel legs (2 to 3 oz. each), cleaned and rinsed
 1 cup all-purpose flour
 1 teaspoon Adobo seasoning
 1 cup vegetable oil, approx.

For Stovetop or Surface Cooking: Pierce squirrel legs with a fork to tenderize. Dip legs quickly in water to moisten slightly. Combine flour and Adobo seasoning in dish, stirring to mix well. Coat squirrel legs with seasoned flour, shaking off any excess. In heavy-bottomed large skillet, heat about 1/2 inch of oil over medium-high heat. When hot, add squirrel legs. Fry until golden brown on all sides.

VENISON-A-RONI

LAYNE KINGE, BRIGHTON, TENNESSEE

Born in Caribou, Maine, and raised along the Atlantic seacoast, Navy Master Chief Kinge has also spent a lot of time in the Hatchie River basin of Tennessee, where deer are plentiful enough to provide this delicious dish often. It makes a great lunch even if you're on a one-day deer hunting trip. Pack along a small frying pan and the few necessary ingredients in your backpack. Fresh venison will never taste so good!

Serves: 3 to 4
Cooking Time: Under 30 minutes

    White-tailed deer tenderloin (about 1 lb.)
    Water
 2 tablespoons vegetable oil
 1 box (6.8 oz.) beef Rice-A-Roni®
    Salt and pepper

For Stovetop or Surface Cooking: Remove tenderloin from a freshly killed deer. Rinse with fresh water and slice into quarter-sized pieces about 1/2 inch thick. Heat oil in skillet over a hot flame. Add venison and brown for about 1 minute on each side. Add Rice-A-Roni and prepare according to package directions. Salt and pepper to taste. This is good with a vegetable like green beans or corn.

CAMPFIRE STEW

MICHELLE MOSURE, SASKATOON, SASKATCHEWAN, CANADA

Michelle is a native of Saskatchewan and has been fishing the province's lakes since she was very young. During the warmer summer months, she and her husband, Dean, pack up the children and head off to beautiful Deifenbaker Lake for a weekend of camping. Here's one of Michelle's camp favorites.

Serves: 6 to 8
Cooking Time: 30 to 60 minutes

2 lbs. ground beef
2 large onions, cut into pieces
4 potatoes, cut into chunks
1 lb. baby carrots (or cut whole carrots)
   Salt and pepper
   You will also need: Heavy-duty aluminum foil, grill grate

For Cooking Over Coals: Prepare campfire or grill. Tear off 6 to 8 large pieces of heavy-duty aluminum foil. Roll ground beef into small balls and divide evenly between pieces of foil. Add onions, potatoes and carrots; sprinkle with salt and pepper to taste. Wrap packets by bringing together the longer sides of the foil and folding the edges together down toward the center (make at least 2 folds); then roll-fold ends in tightly, making 2 or 3 folds. Place on grate over fire. Cook for about 30 minutes, turning occasionally; depending upon the fire, they may need a bit more or less cooking time.

BBQ MUSTARD-DILL SALMON

HANS L. IMFELD, SAN JOSE, CALIFORNIA

Hans is a member of the Outdoorsman's Edge book club and submitted this recipe for one of our contests. As you can see, he knows how to cook up a good fish.

Serves: 4 to 6
Cooking Time: Under 30 minutes

1/4 cup Dijon mustard
 2 tablespoons extra-virgin olive oil
 2 tablespoons dry white wine
 1 clove garlic, minced

2- to 3-lb. salmon fillet, boned but with skin on
    Dry dill weed
    Salt and pepper
    You will also need: Grill grate, cooking spray

For Cooking Over Coals: Prepare campfire or grill. Spray grill grate with cooking spray; set aside. In small bowl, combine mustard, olive oil, wine and garlic. Spread mustard mixture over flesh side of salmon. Sprinkle liberally with dill weed; season with salt and pepper to taste. Place grate over cooler coals (if using gas grill, lower heat to medium-low). Place fillet on grate, skin side down. Cook for 20 to 25 minutes, or until fish flakes easily with fork.

Note: The tail end of the fish will cook more quickly, and will be done after about 10 minutes of cooking. It makes a great appetizer for the chef until the rest of the fish is done!

LINDA'S SOUTHERN-FRIED RABBIT

DAVID AND LINDA FISHER, SMITHFIELD, PENNSYLVANIA

The author of several books on rabbit hunting (including his latest work, Outdoorsman's Edge Guide to Cottontail Rabbit Hunting), Dave Fisher happily supplied this recipe to share with my readers. He's a pro at what he does and this recipe makes for some mighty delicious rabbit eating. The gravy is excellent over mashed potatoes. Chicken was never this good!

Serves: 4 to 6

Cooking Time: Over 3 hours

1¹/₂ cups vegetable oil

  2 dressed wild rabbits* (about 2 lbs. total; preferably young), cut into quarters

1¹/₂ cups all-purpose flour

  6 chicken bouillon cubes

  4 cups water, divided

¹/₂ teaspoon paprika

¹/₂ teaspoon garlic powder

   Salt and pepper

For Stovetop or Surface Cooking: In large, deep skillet or Dutch Oven, heat oil over medium-high heat. Coat rabbit pieces with flour and brown well; reserve remaining flour. Remove rabbit and set aside. Remove skillet from heat and add bouillon cubes. Stir to dissolve bouillon cubes, and set skillet aside for a few minutes.

When oil is slightly cooler, add 2 cups water (be careful to avoid any spattering) and the reserved flour, stirring constantly to remove any lumps. Return to heat and add the remaining 2 cups water, stirring constantly. Stir in paprika, garlic powder, and salt and pepper to taste. Add more water, if necessary, to make enough gravy to cover the rabbit pieces. Lower heat to simmering and return rabbit to skillet. Cover and simmer for about 3 hours, or until rabbit is tender when forked.

*Dave's note: I always cut my rabbits in fours for ease of preparation. Then, I make sure they are cleaned, rinsed and soaked in a salt brine solution overnight. Remove rabbit pieces from the salt brine and pat dry before cooking.

Release the Hounds!

☞ *When hunting cottontails, wait in the area where the dogs first detect fresh scent. A rabbit will usually circle and return to the spot where it was flushed. If it does not circle, try to predict its escape route, then attempt to intercept it.*

☞ *Beagles are popular dogs for hunting rabbits. They have excellent noses and will scour the ground thoroughly to find fresh scent. They will methodically follow the trail, slowly pushing the rabbit ahead.*

DEER CAMP STEW

FRANK LUCA, STATEN ISLAND, NY

Peter and I have shared many meals at camp while deer hunting with Frank in Hancock, New York. Frank is an ardent deer hunter. Over the years, he has developed many delicious recipes that are enjoyed by everyone at the lodge. This recipe surpasses all.

<u>Serves:</u> 8
<u>Cooking Time:</u> Over 3 hours

1/4 cup vegetable oil, divided
2 lbs. boneless venison, cut into stew-sized cubes
5 cups sliced onions
1 can (6 oz.) tomato paste

2 cups beer (1 pint), approx.
3 potatoes, cubed
3 carrots, cut into 2-inch chunks
1 bay leaf
Salt and pepper

<u>For Stovetop or Surface Cooking:</u> In stockpot or Dutch oven, heat 2 tablespoons of the oil over high heat. Brown venison on all sides. Transfer browned venison to dish; set aside. Add onions and remaining 2 tablespoons oil to pot. Cook for 5 minutes, stirring occasionally. Return venison to pot, placing it on top of onions. Add tomato paste. Add enough beer to just cover venison. Reduce heat to medium-low, cover pot and cook for 2 hours. Add potatoes, carrots and bay leaf. Cook for 45 minutes longer, or until potatoes and carrots are soft. Remove bay leaf. Season with salt and pepper to taste.

SMYTH-BEEKMAN "INTERNATIONALLY FAMOUS" BLUE-CLAW CRAB SPREAD

PATTY BEEKMAN, FRASER, COLORADO

My sister, Patty, has long enjoyed the outdoors through her passions for horseback riding, skiing, outdoor photography and snowmobiling. She passed along this recipe; it is one of her favorites that is quick and easy to prepare. This is a great crowd-pleaser and makes an excellent appetizer.

<u>Serves:</u> 8
<u>Cooking Time:</u> Under 15 minutes

2 packages (8 oz. each) cream cheese
1 lb. cooked blue-claw crab or crawfish meat, chopped
1 bunch of scallions, chopped

1/8 teaspoon Worcestershire sauce
1/8 teaspoon lemon juice
Soy sauce to taste
Crackers for serving

<u>No Cooking Required:</u> In mixing bowl, combine all ingredients except crackers and mix well. Serve with crackers (the best are Triscuits).

Deer Camp Memories

☞ *For many hunters, deer camp is a place you go only once a year, during the gun deer season. This is unfortunate, as deer camps can also serve as a home base for summer fishing outings, early fall bear hunting adventures and winter snowmobiling trips. This year, plan to spend more time at deer camp. You'll be glad you did.*

BAKED FRESHWATER FISH

LAURIER HOULE, SASKATCHEWAN, CANADA

Laurier is a talented taxidermist who has been providing museum-quality mounts for clients since 1972. He also has a great passion for cooking fish and wild game. Here's one of his favorite recipes.

Serves: 2 or 3
Cooking Time: 30 to 60 minutes

1 cup all-purpose flour
1 cup crushed cornflake cereal
  Butter, oil or cooking spray
1 lb. skinless freshwater fish fillets,
  1/4 inch thick, cut into bite-sized cubes*

1/2 cup lemon juice
2 eggs, beaten
2 tablespoons Cajun seasoning

For Camp or Home Cooking in an Oven: Heat oven to 450°F. Sprinkle flour and crushed cornflakes on a baking sheet; set aside. Grease a shallow baking dish generously with butter, oil or cooking spray; set aside. In nonreactive bowl, combine fish cubes and lemon juice, stirring gently to coat. Marinate for 5 minutes, stirring once. After marinating, dip cubes into beaten eggs. As you remove cubes from egg, season with Cajun seasoning and place on prepared baking sheet. Press all sides of the fish firmly into the cornflake mixture. Transfer breaded cubes to prepared baking dish. Bake for 20 to 30 minutes, turning cubes halfway through.

*If you like, you can prepare this dish using whole fillets rather than cubes.

CAMP POPOVERS

ELIZABETH BOTZOW-MCKINNON, CENTER CONWAY, NEW HAMPSHIRE

Elizabeth is a long-time friend who loves the outdoors as much as I do. My early teens were spent hiking, skiing, canoeing, and camping in the unspoiled outdoors of the Northeast (does the Jersey Shore count?) with Elizabeth and her family. Now Elizabeth shares that love of the outdoors with her own family around their home in the pristine mountains of northern New Hampshire. If your camp has an oven, you'll definitely want to make these. Serve them with your favorite soup or jam.

Yield: 6 popovers
Cooking Time: Over 1 hour

  Cooking spray, butter or shortening
4 large eggs
1 1/3 cups milk

1 1/3 cups flour
1/4 teaspoon salt
5 tablespoons butter, melted

For Camp or Home Cooking in an Oven: Heat oven to 375°F. Grease large-cup muffin tin; set aside. In mixing bowl, combine eggs, milk, flour and salt. Begin beating with wire whisk; while beating, pour melted butter into bowl in a steady stream. Beat until well mixed, but don't overbeat. Pour batter into prepared tin. Bake for 45 to 60 minutes. No dancing in the camp kitchen while popovers are popping!

Note: The trick in getting them to pop? Make sure your oven is preheated, and don't overmix the batter.

DAVID HUGHES' OUTRAGEOUS POTATOES

DAVID HUGHES, NEW YORK, NEW YORK

David is the supervising editorial director for one of Bookspan's outdoor book clubs, On The Rise — a fly fishing club. He is also a passionate actor and artist. When he originally shared this recipe with me, we were discussing the watercolor art exhibition of Mari Lyons, wife of legendary fly fishing author Nick Lyons, as David recently expanded his artisan talents to include watercolor as well. After trying this recipe, you'll see evidence of his other talent and passion: cooking.

<u>Serves:</u> 6 to 8
<u>Cooking Time:</u> 1 1/2 hours

3/4 cup butter (1 1/2 sticks), divided, plus additional for greasing pot
1 small to medium head of cabbage, quartered and thinly sliced
2 large Vidalia onions, thinly sliced; or enough wild onions to make about 4 cups
6 Yukon gold potatoes
2 quarts water, approx.
  Salt
1/2 to 3/4 cup milk
  Black pepper
  You will also need: Dutch oven, aluminum foil

For Dutch Oven Cooking: In Dutch oven, melt 1 stick of the butter over medium heat. Add cabbage and onions, stirring to combine. Cook until cabbage and onions turn a deep brown color, stirring frequently at first and then occasionally. (This could take about 45 minutes — but it's worth it.) Meanwhile, prepare campfire.

Peel and cut potatoes into 1- to 2-inch chunks. Boil in salted water until tender. Drain and mash with the milk and the remaining 1/4 cup of butter until creamy. Season with pepper. Stir in one-half of the cabbage mixture.

Preheat Dutch oven lid in coals. Rub some butter on the inside bottom and about 2 inches up the insides of the Dutch oven. Place potato-cabbage mixture into Dutch oven. Top with remaining cabbage mixture. Place preheated lid on Dutch oven. Position Dutch oven over small bed of coals; place additional hot coals on top of lid. Bake for about 20 minutes, or until heated through.

For Camp or Home Cooking in an Oven: Heat oven to 350°F. Prepare cabbage mixture and mashed potatoes as directed above. Combine mashed potatoes with half of the cabbage mixture, and place in casserole dish. Top with remaining cabbage mixture. Cover casserole and bake for 15 to 20 minutes, or until heated through.

Lessons to Learn

☞ *Several years ago, during a camp-out in Wyoming, I met some hunters who had started their campfire too close to the surrounding trees. The flames from this mini-bonfire were licking the pine branches hanging above. Fortunately, members of our party politely pointed out their serious oversight and helped them move the fire to a better and safer location. Another time, on a fishing trip in New Hampshire, a young woman was washing her dishes with regular dish soap in a stream known for its excellent smallmouth bass fishing. Thankfully, our*

continued on page 113

WILD TURKEY BREAST ALMONDINE

PAT AND ERIC BROOKER, ROCHESTER, NEW HAMPSHIRE

Eric is a long-time friend of ours who has been with Thompson Center Arms for many years; we've shared some wonderful hunts for big game and turkey with him. One year, Eric came down to hunt turkeys with us during a spring heat wave in New York. We were joking that we didn't think these birds would come in to Peter's calls, as they more likely would be doing the backstroke in the old mineshaft ponds to cool off. But, as Murphy's law dictates, Eric and Peter returned from their opening-morning hunt before 11:00 a.m. with Eric's first Eastern gobbler.

The heat did not let up, however, and on Eric's 6-hour trip back to New Hampshire, the thermostat blew in his old truck. With the heat turned up all the way, the fans at full blast, and with steadfast determination to pull into his driveway without a tow truck, Eric's only way to cool off while driving was to douse himself with bottled water every few miles or so! I'm sure he and his wife, Pat, had much to reminisce about as they prepared this memorable gobbler!

Serves: 2 or 3
Cooking Time: Under 30 minutes

4 to 6 slices bacon
2 or 3 medium onions, sliced
1 cup roasted almond slivers
1 or 2 cloves garlic
2 boneless, skinless wild turkey breasts

For Stovetop or Surface Cooking: In skillet, fry bacon over medium heat until crisp; remove, crumble and set aside. Add onions, almonds and garlic to skillet. Cook, stirring frequently, until onions are tender; if the garlic turns golden brown before the onions are cooked through, remove garlic and set aside. When onions are cooked through, transfer mixture to a dish and set aside.

Keep bacon drippings warm in skillet over medium-high heat. Slice turkey breasts into 1/4-inch-thick slices. Add to skillet and cook until done, turning once. When all turkey is cooked, rewarm the bacon and the onion mixture and pour over the turkey breast. Delicious!

Note: Depending upon the size of the turkey breasts, the quantities of all other ingredients can be adjusted slightly up or down.

continued from page 112

encounter was amicable and she apologized for her error. I gave her some of my biodegradable soap and told her how to do this properly — and away from water sources. Yet another time, there was the late-summer trip when we encountered bikers in the Sangre de Cristo mountains of New Mexico who were drinking water straight from a stream. They were sure the water was safe because they were in the mountains and the ice-cold water was clear and fast-running. It wasn't until we pointed out that there were free-ranging cattle in the area and there was a good chance that the water was not safe to drink, that they realized their error. I don't know if they got sick or not, but I know they departed knowing the potential hazards of drinking untreated water.

DESSERTS & DRINKS
CAMP RECIPES

*M*aking desserts was one of my earliest cooking passions. In fact, during my early teens, my family dubbed me the Chocolate Fudge Chef. I learned the fine art of fudge making from my Grammie B. I remember her telling me how important temperature was and showing me how to do the "drop-ball" test with the fudge. Her own dessert talents included hand-dipped chocolates and fruits, cakes, pies, more fudge and an endless variety of cookies. This passion carried over into my choice of electives at Cornell University's Hotel School. My favorite class was Desserts. I savored making such rich delights as cream puffs, éclairs, truffles, petit fours, and chocolate mousse cakes. My college roommate was an avowed chocoholic, and the day I brought home a Death by Chocolate cake, she thought she had, in fact, died and gone to heaven!

At camp, most people don't expect to savor the mealtime "extras" they get at home – desserts, a chilled glass of wine, or a specialty tea or coffee. But why not? Appetites – particularly dessert cravings – seem to swell when we're exposed to fresh outdoor air. Satisfying those cravings, and treating yourself and your fellow campers to a few food luxuries, doesn't have to be labor-intensive. In this section you'll find easy no-bake cookies, fast fudge, spicy camp snacks and even some inspiring ideas for using wild berries. Rounding out the chapter are some recipes for special coffee and tea drinks that will break up the the routine of regular ol' cowboy coffee or reconstituted powdered soft drinks and lend a pampered air to your camp or cabin with little effort.

APPALACHIAN TRAIL FUDGE

This is a great, quick dessert that can be whipped up after lunch or dinner for a sweet treat – providing just the energy boost your fellow campers need after a long day in the outdoors.

Serves: 2 or 3
Cooking Time: Under 15 minutes

1/2 cup mini marshmallows, or 4 regular-sized marshmallows, chopped
3 tablespoons butter
2 tablespoons chunky peanut butter
1/4 cup plain M&Ms candies
3 tablespoons instant hot chocolate mix
3 tablespoons water
2 tablespoons powdered milk
Plain graham crackers, optional

For Stovetop or Surface Cooking: In nonstick pan, combine marshmallows, butter and peanut butter. Heat over low heat until marshmallows melt, stirring frequently. Add M&Ms, hot chocolate mix, water and powdered milk; stir to mix thoroughly. Spoon onto plate in large dollops and eat warm, or dollop onto graham crackers and enjoy!

CINNAMON-RAISIN-NUT TWISTS

Who says you can't have fresh-baked pastries at camp and still have time to take in the sunset? These will have everyone asking for seconds.

<u>Yield:</u> 16 twists
<u>Cooking Time:</u> 30 to 60 minutes

Topping:
1/4 cup packed brown sugar
1/4 cup chopped walnuts
1/4 cup raisins, chopped after measuring
 1 tablespoon cinnamon

2 tubes (8 oz. each) refrigerated crescent rolls
3 tablespoons butter, softened
 You will also need: Dutch oven, aluminum foil

<u>Optional Advance Preparation:</u> Combine topping ingredients in plastic food-storage bag.

<u>For Dutch Oven Cooking:</u> Prepare campfire; preheat Dutch oven lid in coals. Line inside bottom of Dutch oven with foil; set aside. Unroll both tubes of crescent rolls on a clean, flat work surface (or one covered with foil). Press seams together on each piece of dough so that you have 2 solid rectangles of dough. Spread butter on each dough rectangle. Sprinkle topping mixture evenly over both dough rectangles. Lightly press topping into dough. Fold each piece of dough in half over itself, topping side in. Cut each into 8 strips. Twist each strip and shape into a knot. Place a single layer of knots into prepared Dutch oven (you need to bake these in batches). Place preheated lid on Dutch oven. Position Dutch oven over small bed of coals; place additional hot coals on top of lid. Bake for 12 to 15 minutes, or until golden brown. Repeat with remaining knots.

<u>For Camp or Home Cooking in an Oven:</u> Heat oven to 375°F. Prepare knot-shaped pastries as directed above, arranging on ungreased baking sheet. Bake for 10 to 12 minutes, or until golden brown.

CORN BREAD SWEET TREATS

This dessert/snack is one I'll often prepare toward the end of a trip. It requires no perishables, yet it fills the need for a quick sweet bite.

<u>Serves:</u> 6
<u>Cooking Time:</u> Under 15 minutes

1 1/2 cups cornmeal
 1/4 teaspoon salt
1 1/2 cups boiling water

1/2 cup vegetable oil, approx.
1/2 cup maple syrup or honey

<u>For Stovetop or Surface Cooking:</u> In small bowl, combine cornmeal and salt. Slowly add boiling water, stirring constantly with a spoon until thoroughly combined. Heat 1/8 to 1/4 inch of cooking oil in large skillet or Dutch oven over medium-high heat. When oil is warm, spoon cornmeal mixture into skillet in 6 mounds. Flatten mounds slightly. Cook for 2 to 3 minutes on each side, or until golden. Drain on paper towels. Drizzle with maple syrup or honey; serve warm.

Powdered Milk

☞ *Powdered dry milk is usually found in boxes in the baking aisle at most grocery stores; it's sometimes referred to as instant dry milk. If you're on an extended trip, carry nonfat powdered milk rather than regular powdered milk, which has more fat and is more prone to spoilage. For carrying to camp, I generally transfer the milk powder to a plastic food-storage bag and write the conversion on the outside of the bag with a black plastic marker: "1 cup milk = 1/3 cup powdered milk plus 1 cup water."*

Keep in mind that due to its reduced fat content, the nonfat milk powder will not have as many calories in it as the whole-milk powder.

NILLA PIE BOWL

While this recipe is delicious just the way it is, you can easily come up with many variations. You can crumble graham crackers, Oreos or chocolate chip cookies over it; use a different flavor of pudding; or top with a few more chopped items like nuts, raisins or chocolate morsels. Have fun with this one! It's been a favorite standby in my camp for many years.

Serves: 4
Preparation Time: Under 15 minutes

   1 package (6 oz.) instant vanilla pudding mix* (I use Jell-O brand)
1/2 cup powdered milk
21/2 cups cold water
 12 Nilla wafer cookies, crushed

Preparation: In mixing bowl or small saucepan, blend together pudding mixture and powdered milk. Add water and mix with a fork or whisk; stir for 2 or 3 minutes. Divide evenly among 4 bowls. Sprinkle the crushed cookies over the top. Serve.

*The instant vanilla pudding mix and powdered milk can be combined in a zipper-style plastic bag at home and labeled as such. Also, this can be prepared by simply pouring the water into the bag, sealing it shut and then mixing the ingredients by shaking and squeezing the bag.

FRIED CINNAMON PITAS

Here's a genuinely quick and easy sweet treat that can be made any time of day. It's sure to please all.

Serves: 4 to 6
Cooking Time: Under 15 minutes

 1 cup sugar*
 2 tablespoons cinnamon*
 3 pocket-style pita breads
1/4 cup vegetable oil

Optional Advance Preparation: Combine sugar and cinnamon in plastic food-storage bag.

For Stovetop or Surface Cooking: If you haven't premixed the sugar and cinnamon, combine them in a dish and mix well. Cut pita pockets open and then slice them into 1-inch-wide strips. In Dutch oven, heat oil over high heat. When oil is sizzling, add several pita strips. Cook until golden brown on both sides, turning as needed. When done, drain briefly on paper towel. While still hot, dunk the sticks in the cinnamon/sugar mix and enjoy!

Note: As noted, you can mix the sugar/cinnamon at home. You might want to mix a double batch, since it's also good as a bread, pancake or toast topping, and is tasty sprinkled on apples.

IN-THE-WILD POPCORN

Oftentimes when I am cooking in bear country, I envision a "Yogi Bear"-type critter picking up the aromas that are wafting from the cookstove and following the aroma right into camp. That's why I like to cook popcorn only when there's some daylight left and I can still see what creatures may be lurking just outside camp. Still, it's the perfect snack food for camp. Here's my popping method, along with some great alternatives to the classic butter topping.

<u>Yield:</u> 8 cups, to serve 2 or 3
<u>Cooking Time:</u> Under 15 minutes

  2 tablespoons oil
1/4 cup popcorn kernels
     Salt to taste
     Flavored topping (optional, recipes below)

<u>For Stovetop or Surface Cooking:</u> Add oil and a single kernel of popcorn to a pot or Dutch oven. Cover pot and heat over medium-high heat. When the kernel pops, open the lid and add remaining popcorn. Re-cover pot and return to heat. When kernels start to pop, make sure you continually shake the pot to keep the kernels moving and popping. From time to time, vent the lid slightly to let some of the steam out. Be careful, as the steam can be dangerous. When the popping starts to slow down, remove from heat, vent the lid slightly and let the remaining hot kernels pop by themselves. Pour into large serving bowl and salt to taste.

Here are some fun topping ideas for the popcorn. For each of these variations except the Zowie, pour the melted butter over the popped popcorn and toss well; then add the remaining ingredient(s) and toss again.

ZESTY CHEESE

1/4 cup butter (half of a stick), melted
1/4 cup grated Parmesan cheese
  1 teaspoon garlic salt

ZINGER

1/4 cup butter (half of a stick), melted
1/8 teaspoon cayenne pepper

RANCH-SIDE

1/4 cup butter (half of a stick), melted
1/2 to 1 tablespoon dried ranch
     dressing mix

ZOWIE

1/4 cup butter (half of a stick)
     Several dashes of Tabasco sauce

In small saucepan, melt butter and add Tabasco sauce. You be the judge as to how much to add! Pour mixture over the popcorn and toss to coat evenly.

Hot-Weather Hunts

☞ *When the weather turns unexpectedly warm during a fall hunting trip, remember that the superb insulating properties of sleeping bags and down jackets will also work to keep items cool while at camp.*

☞ *In much of the West, creek bottoms (both wet and dry) are often deep and well protected from the hot sun. As a result, these areas get cold at night and stay relatively cool during the day. On a hot-weather hunt, hang your harvested game in one of these low bottoms instead of on the higher prairie.*

BAKED APPLES

Some of the best baked apples I prepared were during a fall fishing trip to the Finger Lakes region of New York State. We were spending a long weekend fishing for trout in Cayuga Lake (near my alma mater, Cornell University). I brought along some Cortland apples and made this delicious treat. If you have some cream on hand, warm some up to serve over the apples . . . heavenly.

Wine Bottle "Chopper"

....

☞ *When at camp or at home, an easy way to get "chopped" nuts is to place them in a plastic bag and crush with a rolling pin or wine bottle. It's quick and easy, and there's no messy cutting board to clean later. This way, you can bring whole nuts for snacking and then quickly crush them for recipes as needed.*

Serves: 5
Cooking Time: 1^1/$_2$ hours

Stuffing Mixture:
^{1}/$_4$ cup chopped walnuts
^{1}/$_4$ cup chopped raisins
^{1}/$_4$ cup chopped dried apricots
^{1}/$_4$ cup brown sugar
^{1}/$_2$ teaspoon cinnamon

   5 large apples
   2 tablespoons butter, cut into 5 equal pieces
^{3}/$_4$ cup boiling water
      You will also need: Dutch oven, aluminum foil

Optional Advance Preparation: Combine stuffing-mixture ingredients in plastic food-storage bag.

For Dutch Oven Cooking: Prepare campfire; preheat Dutch oven lid in coals. Line inside bottom of Dutch oven with foil. Core apples, saving ^{1}/$_4$ to ^{1}/$_2$ inch of the bottom of each core; use these to "plug" the bottom of each apple. Make a cut in the apple skin around the "equator" of the apple. Don't cut deeply into the flesh of the apple, just deep enough to cut the skin. Divide stuffing mixture between apples, stuffing into the hollow centers. Place stuffed apples into prepared Dutch oven. Top each apple with a pat of butter. Add boiling water to Dutch oven. Place preheated lid on Dutch oven. Position Dutch oven over small bed of coals; place additional hot coals on top of lid. Bake for 40 to 50 minutes, replenishing coals as necessary. Serve warm, drizzling some of the cooking juices over each apple.

For Camp or Home Cooking in an Oven: Heat oven to 350°F. Stuff apples as directed above, placing them into a glass casserole dish. Cover and bake for 40 to 50 minutes.

WILD BLUEBERRY COBBLER

There's nothing more satisfying to me than picking fresh blueberries and bringing them back to camp to prepare fabulous desserts. That is, of course, if you can pack more blueberries in a pail than you can eat while gathering them!

Serves: 5
Cooking Time: 30 to 60 minutes, plus cooling time

4 cups wild blueberries	1/4 cup butter (half of a stick), melted
Half of a lemon, optional	1 egg, beaten
1 1/2 tablespoons sugar/cinnamon mix*	1 cup milk
1 1/2 tablespoons all-purpose flour	1/2 teaspoon vanilla
2 cups buttermilk baking mix	You will also need: Dutch oven
1/2 cup sugar	

For Dutch Oven Cooking: Prepare campfire; preheat Dutch oven lid in coals. In mixing bowl or large plastic bag, combine blueberries, the juice from the lemon half (if using), sugar/cinnamon mix, and flour. Pour into large Dutch oven. Combine remaining ingredients in mixing bowl and stir well to remove any large lumps. Pour batter over blueberries. Place preheated lid on Dutch oven. Position Dutch oven over small bed of coals; place additional hot coals on top of lid. Bake for 30 to 40 minutes. Cool before serving.

For Camp or Home Cooking in an Oven: Heat oven to 350°F. Prepare blueberries and batter as described above, assembling in large casserole dish. Bake, uncovered, for 45 minutes. Cool before serving.

*Note: You can mix the sugar/cinnamon in a larger amount at home and carry in a zipper-style plastic bag to camp. It's good as a bread, pancake or toast topping, and is tasty sprinkled on apples. To prepare just the quantity used in this recipe, mix a few dashes of cinnamon and 1 1/2 tablespoons sugar.

GRANDMA'S NO-BAKE COOKIES

A quick after-lunch or after-dinner dessert for all.

Yield: About 2 dozen cookies
Cooking Time: Under 15 minutes, plus cooling time

Oatmeal mixture:

2 cups oatmeal	1 cup white sugar
1 cup semi-sweet chocolate morsels	1 cup packed brown sugar
1/2 cup chopped nuts (walnuts, peanuts or pecans)	1/2 cup butter (1 stick)
1/4 cup raisins	1/2 cup milk
	You will also need: Aluminum foil or baking sheet

Optional Advance Preparation: Combine oatmeal-mixture ingredients in plastic food-storage bag. In a separate bag, combine white and brown sugars.

For Stovetop or Surface Cooking: In saucepan, combine white sugar, brown sugar, butter and milk. Heat to boiling over medium-high heat; boil for 1 minute, stirring occasionally. Remove from heat and stir in the oatmeal mixture. Drop in cookie-size globs on a large piece of foil or baking sheet. Cool before serving.

RICE PUDDING

Rice pudding is a nice warm dessert for the days when the weather turns a bit foul. It's not bad on sunny days, either!

Serves: 3 or 4
Cooking Time: Under 15 minutes

Rice mixture:
   1 cup instant rice
 $1/2$ cup raisins
 $1/2$ cup packed brown sugar
 $1/4$ cup powdered milk
   1 teaspoon cinnamon

$2 1/4$ cups water
 $1/2$ teaspoon vanilla

Optional Advance Preparation: Combine rice-mixture ingredients in plastic food-storage bag.

For Stovetop or Surface Cooking: In small pot, heat water to a full boil over high heat. Add rice mixture, stirring to combine. Reduce heat and simmer for 5 minutes, or until rice is done. Add vanilla and stir to mix thoroughly. Serve warm.

MOCHA TRAIL COFFEE

The ever-necessary camp staple — chocolate — adds a delicious flavor to coffee. Don't be surprised if someone exclaims, "Who ordered Starbucks?"

Yield: Enough mix for 25 to 30 servings
Cooking Time: Under 15 minutes

1 cup powdered coffee creamer
1 cup instant coffee
2 packages (1 oz. each) rich chocolate instant cocoa mix

Advance Preparation: Combine all ingredients in either a plastic food-storage bag or plastic container.

For Stovetop or Surface Cooking: Boil 1 cup water per serving. In mug, combine 1 cup boiling water with 1 to $1 1/2$ tablespoons of the coffee mixture. Add sugar to taste, if need be.

Morning Coffee

☞ *Here's a simple recipe that uses tea infusers to help keep the coffee grounds away from your lips!*

In a saucepan, heat 2 cups of water to boiling. While waiting, spoon 1 tablespoon of ground coffee into a tea ball infuser. After the water reaches a boil, hang the tea ball in a mug and add 1 cup of boiling water. Let it brew for about 5 minutes. Remove the tea ball and you'll have minimal grounds in your coffee. Add sugar to your coffee as preferred.

WILD MINT ICED TEA

Mint tea seems to offer a soothing effect to those who imbibe it. Here's a natural way to make a sun-steeped version.

Serves: 4
Preparation Time: Worth the wait

1 quart water
8 stalks wild mint with leaves, rinsed thoroughly
4 tea bags

No Cooking Required: In large glass container, combine all ingredients. Seal with lid. Let steep in the sun for several hours throughout the day. Remove the mint and tea bags and serve over ice.

TANGY HOT PEACH TEA

This zesty drink will surely be an early morning eye-opener!

Yield: Enough mix for 16 servings
Cooking Time: Under 15 minutes

1 cup sweetened peach-flavored instant tea mix
1 cup Tang breakfast drink

1 teaspoon cinnamon
1 teaspoon allspice

Advance Preparation: Combine all ingredients in either a plastic food-storage bag or plastic container.

For Stovetop or Surface Cooking: Boil 1 cup water per serving. In mug, combine 1 cup boiling water with 2 tablespoons of the tea mixture.

CAMP CHAI TEA

If you frequent any of the chain coffee or tea franchises, you'll recognize the term Chai tea. It's a zesty alternative to regular tea and, if your tastes are like mine, this new flavor can be quite pleasantly addictive.

Yield: 8 cups
Cooking Time: Under 30 minutes

Spice Mixture:

1/4 teaspoon ground pepper
1/4 teaspoon ground ginger
3/4 teaspoon ground cardamom
1/4 teaspoon ground cloves
1/4 teaspoon cinnamon

2 quarts water
9 tea bags (orange pekoe works best)
Sugar or honey for serving, optional

Advance Preparation: Combine all spice-mixture ingredients in small plastic food-storage bag.

For Stovetop or Surface Cooking: In large saucepan, heat water to boiling. Remove from heat and stir in the spice mixture. Add tea bags and let steep for 7 minutes. Serve hot and flavor with sugar or honey.

Nutritional Information

If a recipe has a range of servings, the data below applies to the greater number of servings. If the recipe lists a quantity range for an ingredient, the average quantity was used to calculate the nutritional data. In recipes that call for "vension" without specifying what type, deer venison was assumed. If alternate ingredients are listed, the analysis applies to the first ingredient.

	Calories	Protein (g)	Fat (g)	Saturated Fat (g)	Carbohydrate (g)	Sodium (mg)	Cholesterol (mg)
Breakfasts							
Outback Hashbrowns	398	9	19	3	51	169	8
Venison Hash	410	39	12	3	36	229	180
Dutch Oven Sticky Buns	464	6	20	8	66	662	26
Kick-Start Oatmeal	371	8	11	1	66	13	0
Catskill Corn Patties	119	2	4	1	18	253	10
Gobbler Omelet	606	46	44	19	4	600	645
Vegetarian Pita Delight	325	13	18	4	27	406	319
Steak 'n' Fried Eggs	345	33	19	10	8	241	340
Largemouth Scramble	231	19	16	7	2	213	276
Border-Style Scrambled Eggs	628	44	36	10	32	795	430
Brookies 'n' Bacon	577	31	34	11	34	370	95
Skewer Snake River Rainbow Trout	340	44	15	4	4	272	123
Quail with Eggs	988	70	59	15	39	415	625
Kenai River Salmon Frittata	357	28	24	7	6	205	358
El Pike-O Quesadillas	280	19	11	5	24	757	48
Hearty Rocky Mt. Pancakes	150	13	7	3	8	214	45
Creamed Pike over Grits	273	16	9	5	33	692	45
Bueno Burritos	350	27	16	3	23	263	276
Bighorn River Fritters	277	28	13	6	9	138	238
Streamside Salmon 'n' Spuds	344	26	14	2	28	59	62
Walleye Taco Supreme	593	56	29	9	27	498	234
Creamed Turkey on Toast	317	33	11	6	21	328	95
Breads							
Zesty Grilled Garlic Bread	326	11	11	3	46	530	11
Bread-on-a-Stick	286	8	1	.1	60	532	0
Corn Tortillas	93	2	1	.1	20	131	0
Cheddar Biscuits	133	4	6	3	15	197	28
Skillet Bread	330	4	19	3	35	663	0
Light Meals & Sides							
Long Lake Fish Crostini	528	39	27	12	32	493	88
Salmon Croquettes	520	43	30	10	17	425	207
Corn-Row Pheasant Grilled Pizza	1,167	69	58	17	91	1,237	159

	Calories	Protein (g)	Fat (g)	Saturated Fat (g)	Carbohydrate (g)	Sodium (mg)	Cholesterol (mg)
Pheasant Nibbles	491	43	29	16	13	291	161
Wild Chanterelle Mushroom Toast Points	313	4	27	16	16	364	77
Fish Cake Supreme	167	8	10	2	12	281	38
Egg Salad Deluxe	256	13	14	3	18	325	324
Catfish Hoagies	402	26	17	3	34	605	72
Steelhead Chowder	455	30	23	11	32	239	112
Cheesy Corn Chowder	306	15	15	9	30	672	47
Salmon Soup	296	26	7	1	31	1,225	62
Gobbler Soup	208	22	1	.2	27	882	44
Grouse 'n' pea soup	454	39	6	2	63	431	34
Oriental Pheasant Noodle Soup	414	32	15	7	37	948	75
Turkey & Rice Soup	399	33	11	4	39	1,122	80
Wild Rice & Duck Soup	363	17	24	13	22	1,114	94
Chicken Chowder	326	26	14	5	25	727	80
Pesto Pasta Soup	241	8	15	2	21	1.308	2
Rainy Day Venison Chili	449	37	18	6	36	769	112
Duck 'n' Dandelion Salad	406	12	36	8	11	733	42
Pike's Pete Salad	275	38	12	2	2	122	77
Catfish Rice Salad	444	23	17	5	49	1,026	64
Fish & Corn Salad	325	40	6	1	31	657	71
Striper Salad	576	26	49	8	8	571	229
Midday Trout Delight	342	27	20	3	15	547	66
Pharaoh Lake Potato Salad	424	13	21	4	45	673	216
Skillet Potato Patties	116	2	6	2	13	119	1
Tomatoes 'n' Rice	366	9	8	1	67	653	0
Roasted Wild Onions & Mushrooms	194	6	12	7	17	299	31
Grilled Camp Veggies	84	2	6	4	7	221	16
Corn on the Cob	111	3	5	3	17	53	10
Easy Camp Tomato Sauce	44	1	3	.4	5	80	0
Dog 'n' Bean Casserole	490	17	23	8	55	1,497	39
Camp Macaroni & Cheese	873	37	39	24	92	723	116

Main Dishes	Calories	Protein (g)	Fat (g)	Saturated Fat (g)	Carbohydrate (g)	Sodium (mg)	Cholesterol (mg)
Barbecued Mallard Duck Breasts	666	67	29	8	32	230	367
Soy-Grilled Ruffed Grouse	1,444	180	73	21	5	3,070	554
Grilled Quail	1,058	53	89	17	12	1,066	201
Turkey Rolls Supreme	329	19	18	6	20	703	45
Grilled Grouse	1,352	145	81	30	.1	599	502
Baked Pheasant Casserole	1,063	58	83	29	20	1,480	245
Indian Pheasant Stir-Fry	300	39	10	2	14	1,433	88
Sautéed Apple Grouse	950	90	50	12	31	181	277
Fried Quail	963	63	67	29	24	470	312
Southern Fried Quail	859	68	46	10	39	1,001	337
Pan Turkey 'n' Stuffing	421	39	19	11	23	934	135
Fried Goose Breasts	541	54	27	10	16	270	202
Peter Rabbit Stew 'n' Dumplings	605	43	24	6	54	1,196	126
Hedgerow Rabbit Sauté	709	80	31	8	25	605	216
Venison Filet w/ Morels	668	30	49	30	22	600	221
Easy Venison Goulash	535	39	11	2	68	467	96
River Bottom Venison Teriyaki	288	31	3	1	32	1,440	96
Easy Venison Roast	460	55	23	9	5	361	213
Trout-Stuffed Corn Husks	361	35	18	8	17	172	119
Grill-Roasted Striped Bass	237	31	11	2	4	702	136
Salmon Steak Barbecue	206	23	8	1	8	559	62
Garlic Salmon	456	24	36	5	11	514	62
Rainbow Trout & Mushrooms in Foil	565	51	31	16	19	301	191
Stuffed Baked Pike	357	21	28	10	5	577	67
Baked Pike 'n' Potatoes	641	52	27	11	46	396	127
Parmesan Baked Perch	422	36	8	4	50	733	151
Catfish Noodle Bake	519	30	28	10	35	282	104
Walleye Bake Forestiere	351	42	17	8	7	865	213
Walleye in Creamy Bacon-Mushroom Sauce	614	50	30	7	33	857	215
Walleye in Ale	438	45	19	11	19	1,492	251
Poached Salmon Steaks	370	48	16	3	5	1,685	123
Savory Poached Brookies	493	29	36	17	15	466	136
Walleye Cordon Bleu	547	66	24	11	14	1,949	283
Midwest Lobster	744	44	63	38	.5	713	254
Perch Panfry	829	75	34	5	51	245	413
Fried Catfish	404	19	30	11	12	602	77
Sautéed Trout w/ Wild Onions	481	61	15	5	21	140	176

	Calories	Protein (g)	Fat (g)	Saturated Fat (g)	Carbohydrate (g)	Sodium (mg)	Cholesterol (mg)
Pike Crispy Fingers	592	51	24	8	41	202	177
Beer Batter Perch	600	80	18	3	29	1,269	350
Country Crawfish Boil	560	26	35	12	38	2,090	117
Boiled Crawfish	838	6	92	57	.1	952	286
Grilled Lobster	568	32	47	29	5	1,284	232
Outfitters' Best							
Northern Venison Wildlife Popcorn	391	33	19	3	20	67	110
Baked Duck & Rice	898	42	54	16	60	971	163
Pat's Marinated Venison	204	27	10	2	1	573	96
Baked Trout w/ Wild Rice Stuffing	573	50	29	8	21	289	145
Bob's No Cleanup Salmon	435	46	26	9	3	220	156
Thorofare Dutch Oven Breakfast	452	20	20	5	47	167	510
John's Beef Tenderloin	657	35	53	15	10	1,379	112
Readers' Best							
Bill's No-Fail Salmon Sauté	604	38	40	8	23	834	105
Streamside Willow Trout	208	29	9	2	0	73	82
Garlic Venison Cutlets Supreme	693	55	33	8	43	866	253
Fried Squirrel Legs	823	44	61	8	24	376	158
Venison-A-Roni	412	31	16	3	35	838	97
Campfire Stew	531	25	35	14	29	129	110
BBQ Mustard-Dill Salmon	383	45	20	3	.2	388	125
Linda's Southern-Fried Rabbit	889	36	69	9	30	1,226	118
Deer Camp Stew	324	30	10	2	29	245	96
Smyth-Beekman Blue-Claw Crab Spread	261	16	21	13	3	329	119
Baked Freshwater Fish	620	44	16	4	71	2,301	235
Camp Popovers	275	9	16	8	24	262	175
David Hughes' Potatoes	321	6	18	11	37	219	49
Wild Turkey Breast Almondine	741	60	47	11	22	361	143
Desserts							
Cinnamon-Raisin-Nut Twists	162	2	9	3	17	244	6
Appalachian Trail Fudge	341	6	21	8	34	267	35
Corn Bread Sweet Treats	356	3	19	2	44	99	0
Nilla Pie Bowl	239	4	2	.5	53	699	3
Fried Cinnamon Pitas	298	3	10	1	52	162	0
In-The-Wild Popcorn	142	2	10	1	12	.5	0
Baked Apples	260	2	9	3	48	53	12
Wild Blueberry Cobbler	497	8	19	9	74	725	74
Grandma's No-Bake Cookies	184	2	8	4	28	47	11
Rice Pudding	266	4	.2	0	64	38	1

Camp Kitchen Suppliers

Camp Stoves, Ovens, Grills & Accessories

Alco-Brite
P.O. Box 840926
Hildale, UT 84784
www.alco-brite.com

BeaverTree Kitchen
P.O. Box 97
Fall Creek, WI 54742
www.beavertree.com

The Coleman Company – Peak 1
3600 N. Hydraulic
Wichita, KS 67219
www.coleman.com

Fox Hill Corp.
P.O. Box 259
Rozet, WY 82727
www.foxhill.net

Mountain Stream Forge
P.O. Box 262
Canby, OR 97013
www.mountainstreamforge.com

Open Fire Grill
RD 2 Box 315A
Saltsburg, PA 15681
www.openfiregrill.com

Catalog Houses

Cabela's
400 E. Ave. A
Oshkosh, NE 69190
www.cabelas.com

Campmor
P.O. Box 700
Upper Saddle River, NJ 07458
www.campmor.com

Ensley's Shooting Supply
115 Christopher Lane
Louisville, TN 37777
www.ensleys-shooting.com

Forestry Suppliers, Inc.
P.O. Box 8397
Jackson, MS 39284
www.forestry-suppliers.com

Sierra Trading Post
5025 Campstool Road
Cheyenne, WY 82007
www.sierratradingpost.com

Dutch Ovens

Camp Chef
P.O. Box 4057
Logan, UT 84323-4057
www.campchef.com

Chuck Wagon Supply
1230 Fern St.
Pocatello, ID 83201-3008
www.chuckwagonsupply.com

Lodge Manufacturing Co.
P.O. Box 380
South Pittsburg, TN 37380
www.lodgemfg.com

Index